HOPE, GRACE & FAITH

HOPE, GRACE & FAITH

Leah Messer

Post Hill
PRESS

A POST HILL PRESS BOOK
ISBN: 978-1-64293-931-6

Hope, Grace & Faith
© 2020 by Leah Messer
All Rights Reserved

Cover art by Cody Corcoran
Interior design and layout by Sarah Heneghan,
sarah-heneghan.com

Post Hill Press
New York • Nashville
posthillpress.com

Published in the United States of America

To my daughters Aliannah, Aleeah, and Adalynn:
When I was lost you helped me find my way.
You are my reason for everything in life.

To Lindsay Rielly, Larry Musnik, and my MTV family:
Thank you for supporting me when I needed it most.

To all those who have endured
childhood abuse of any kind:
You're one decision away from a different life.
I believe in you.

God grant me courage and hope for everyday
faith to guide me along my way...
and grace to accept what life gives me to do.

—Helen Steiner Rice

TABLE OF CONTENTS

Prologue

WAKING UP FROM A
LONG NIGHTMARE

I keep having the same dream over and over. I'm at the bottom of a deep dark pool of water. I feel a heavy pressure weighing down on my ribs. I need to breathe, but I know instinctively that I can't give in to the urge to gasp for air. Way above me in the distance, I can see a single ray of light piercing through the blackness. I know I need to swim to that light if I want to breathe again—if I want to see my babies again. I kick my legs and pump my arms with all the strength I have in my body. I'm a strong swimmer, but no matter how hard I push against the water, the light above me keeps getting dimmer and farther away. Something—I can't see what—is holding onto me, pulling me down deeper and deeper. I panic and open my mouth to scream for help. I feel my lungs spasm as they fill with water. I realize with terrifying clarity that I am drowning. I reach out into the darkness, searching for

1

something to grab onto that will keep me from falling into the abyss. There's nothing out there but darkness...

I start to realize something is really wrong with me when one of the executive producers tells me that I couldn't keep my eyes open on camera. The crazy thing is, I didn't even know I was that out of it when they were filming. I've been taking a lot of medications, but I'm not a drug addict. After they botched my spinal tap when I was giving birth to my youngest daughter, the hospital discharged me with refill prescriptions for Hydrocodone, Oxycodone, and Tylenol 3, but what really knocked me out was the Diazepam. My doctor prescribed it to calm the free-falling anxiety I experience every time I try to wrap my mind around the stack of medical bills piling up on my kitchen counter. With all the doctor appointments I've been juggling for Ali, my oldest, I never had time to schedule a follow-up appointment to figure out why I'm still in so much pain, so my dad has been hooking me up with the same medications.

Some mornings the spinal headaches are so intense it's a struggle just to get out of bed, but I have three little girls I need to take care of. I keep taking the pills so I can get up, get the twins ready for school, look after my youngest, and face the daily reality of my oldest daughter's diagnosis with a rare form of muscular dystrophy—without completely falling apart. At first, the medications helped dull the pain in my body and my mind, but at some point, they stopped helping. Now, I'm starting to think they might be part of the problem. I just want to feel normal, but I'm either in so much physical pain that I can barely stand, or so foggy from the pills that I look like a junkie. I try taking half the dose, and then a quarter. My doctor keeps telling me that my body will regulate. I'll adjust to the medication and not feel so groggy. The puncture that's leaking spinal fluid into my body will eventually heal and the headaches will go away. Deep down, though, I wonder if I'm so broken there's no medication in the world that can fix me.

I don't know how I got to this place. Sometimes I look around and I don't even recognize my life. It feels like one minute I was a sixteen-year-old cheerleader with dreams of going to college, and then someone pressed fast forward on my life. Now, I'm a twenty-two-year-old single mother of three, sifting through the wreckage of two failed marriages and trying to figure out how I fucked up my life so badly. I've made so many mistakes I've lost count. They keep piling up, like pebbles in a jar, until there's no room left for the person I used to be—or hoped I could become.

I've almost forgotten (or maybe I just don't care anymore) that my life is being recorded for a reality television show and edited for maximum drama. The show has been a part of my life for so long now it's hard to remember what it was like before I had a camera crew following me around, or producers dictating which parts of my life make it onto television and which parts end up on the cutting room floor. I don't really have a choice anyway. I agreed to live in this fishbowl. Between the mortgage on our house, Ali's medical bills, and the money I naively kept lending my dad to help him get back up on his feet, I need the income.

I try to stop taking the medications, but my whole body aches like I have the flu and I feel like I'm going to puke. I tell my mom that I don't feel right. I stay at her house for a few days. She and my stepdad, who's an RN, try to help me wean myself off of the medications. They give me Imodium for the nausea and Tylenol for the body aches. It helps, but I can't hide out at my mom's forever. I go check on my dad, and as I'm leaving, he presses a couple of pills into my hand. I don't want to take them, but I'm in so much pain. I need to keep it together in front of the cameras. I have to pretend I'm okay. If I slip up, even a little, it could give the twins' dad ammunition he could use to get custody of them.

I know the Internet trolls and gossip sites are going to have a field day when this season airs, but I feel so depleted that I'm beyond caring what I look like on camera or how it influences the way other people perceive me. I can already see the headline: "Troubled *Teen Mom* Leah Messer on Drugs as Second Marriage Collapses!" As cruel as the media and bloggers have been, the people who judge me the most harshly are the ones in my own hometown. But they have no idea what my life is really like— the humiliation of millions of people judging me for the stupid mistakes I made as a teenager, the heartache of failing at two marriages, the mind-splintering spinal headaches ever since my youngest was born, the loneliness of taking care of three little girls all on my own, the day-to-day reality of raising a child with special needs whose future is being eclipsed by a condition that I have no control over. They have no idea.

When I think about Ali, I just want to know *why* this is happening to her. She is so sweet and innocent. She deserves to have the same future as her sisters. I want to scream at the world that it isn't fair. I would never wish what Ali has on another child, but why *her*? Why did *she* have to be born into a body that won't have the strength to run along the beach, do a cartwheel, or climb a tree? I'm so sad and angry all the time I can barely eat... or sleep...or breathe. I feel like I'm suffocating. When I close my eyes at night, the voice in my head gets stuck in an endless loop.

Is it my fault?

Is Ali being punished because I'm a bad person?

Am I doing enough to get her the help she needs?

Do I even deserve to be her mother?

Maybe the girls would be better off without me.

I don't even remember getting into my car. I just know that I can barely see the road through the tears streaming down my face. I glance back over my shoulder at the three, crumb-covered car seats behind me. Except for Addie's sippy cup, they're empty. I do a mental check. Ali and Aleeah are with their dad. Addie is spending the night with Jeremy's mom while he's away working. It's just me in the car.

I press my foot down on the gas and watch as the needle on the speedometer goes from 80...to 90...to 110 mph. It's dark and there's no one else on road. I've driven down this stretch of Mink Shoals Hill a thousand times. There's a steep cliff off the side of the road just up ahead. It would be so easy to drive my car over the edge. Then it would all be over. No more worries. No more failure. No more pain.

Instead, I slow down and pull over to the side of the road. I turn off the engine and put my head down on the steering wheel. A lifetime of tears comes pouring out of the deepest part of my soul. I cry so hard I wonder if I'll ever be able to stop. Then a thought cuts through the deafening static in my brain: *My daughters need me.* I take a deep breath and a calming stillness settles over me. It's like I was in the middle of a violent thunderstorm, then suddenly the clouds parted and now everything is bathed in a warm light. I can see clearly what I have to do. *My daughters need me.* It would be selfish to abandon them, to leave them with the same void I've been trying to fill my whole life. For better or worse, I'm all they have.

I need to be stronger. I need to get the hell out of here and fix myself, so I can be the mother that my daughters deserve.

Chapter One:

DADDY'S GIRL

All my life, all I ever wanted was to feel loved. For a long time, I wasn't capable of searching within myself to find that love. So it became this big, empty void that I was always looking for someone else to fill. When I look back at my life, it's so clear to me that I was repeating the same mistakes my mom made—searching for love in the wrong places, getting pregnant at seventeen, dragging my pain from one relationship into the next without ever stopping to unpack any of my baggage. I allowed myself to get pulled into that cycle because I desperately wanted to feel loved, and it took hitting rock bottom for me to realize that if I wanted something better for my girls, I had to learn to love myself first.

When you grow up in a home that's dysfunctional, you end up attracting dysfunction into your life because it's all you know. I don't remember my mom and dad ever

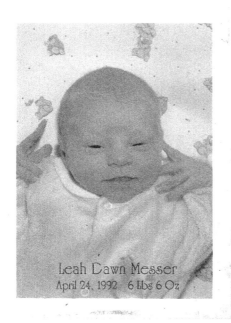

Leah Dawn Messer
April 24, 1992   6 Lbs 6 Oz

being happy to-gether. They must have loved each oth-er in the beginning, but by the time I was two years old, their marriage had become complete-ly toxic. I was five when they finally split up for good, and after that, we moved around so much I never es-tablished a stable home environment. My brother, Isaac, and my sister, Victoria, were too young to understand what was happening, but I was in kinder-garten at the time. I took it really hard. My teacher called my mom to tell her she was worried about me because I had burst into tears when she asked me about the picture I was drawing of me and my dad.

What I remember most from the years before my dad spiraled into drug addiction and my mom kicked him out, is just feeling so close to him. Wherever he went, I wanted to be right there by his side, like his little shadow. When I close my eyes and think back on that period, I see snap-shots of myself curled up in my dad's lap, or him getting down on the floor to play with me. Like moments frozen in time. My earliest memories are of him preaching at our church in Queen Shoals, West Virginia. He worked a day job for a government contractor building bridges for the county, but his true calling was as a Baptist preacher. He knew the Bible like the back of his hand, and back then he was still handsome and full of charm. I remember my mom taking us to watch him preach at an outdoor tent revival in our town one time. I couldn't have been more than three or four years old, but I have a vivid memory of him coming out onto the makeshift stage wearing raggedy pants and a shirt that was all torn up. I didn't really understand all the words he was saying in his sermon, but I knew he was dressed that way to make a point: God loves *all* of his children, no matter what we struggle with or how imperfect we are.

I was sitting in the front row next to Victoria, who was barely out of diapers and more interested in fidgeting around in her chair than the wisdom our daddy was preaching on the stage. I turned around in my seat to look back at the crowd of people sitting behind us in rows of metal folding chairs. They were hanging on my dad's every word, praising Jesus and calling out "Amen!" When I turned back around and looked up at my dad, he was smiling down at me. Even dressed in rags, he had a glow about him. He held out his hand, so I hopped off my chair and walked over to him. I can still remember, so clearly, the feeling of love that washed over me as he pulled me up on stage so I could preach to the congregation right alongside him. That's the last happy memory I have with my dad. According to my mom, he fell in with the wrong crowd, starting smoking weed, and taking pills. The way my dad tells it, he hurt his back working construction and ended up getting hooked on pain medications. Either way, the end result was the same. He became a junkie who could barely take care of himself, much less his wife and children.

I'm not sure my mom has ever gotten over her anger towards him. They met at church when she was sixteen and he was twenty-five. She saw him preaching and was totally in awe. Within a year, they were married and I was born. Nobody really thought twice about the age difference or the fact that my mom had a baby at sixteen. In her family that was just what you did. Growing up, her mother was more interested in making sure my mom helped her with the housework than how she was doing in school. Going to college or having a career wasn't even a consideration. When you grow up in a really small town like ours, the goal for so many young people (especially for women) is to get married and have kids. You're living on the poverty line and there aren't that many options— so you just follow the family cycle.

For my mom, getting married to my dad at sixteen was also a way out of her unhappy home life. Her real father left when she was a baby and her stepdad was a mean drunk who was physically abusive to her and my grandma. They never knew when he was going to snap and become violent. She lost count of how many times their dinner ended up on the floor after he lost his temper and slammed his fists into the table, or how many nights she cried herself to sleep listening to him and my grandma fighting when he came home late after a night of

Me, age four.

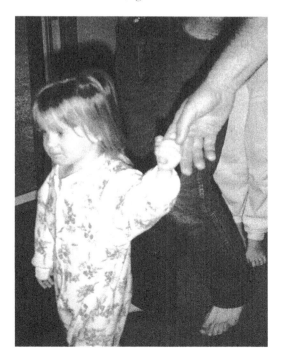

drinking. It always ended with him throwing my grandma against a wall or shoving her into a dresser. The worst story she ever told us was about the time she was playing outside while her stepdad was working on a gas-powered lawnmower. He told her to go and get him a wrench from the garage. When she brought him the wrong kind of tool, he got angry and threw the container of gasoline he was holding in her face. She wanted out of that life, and when my dad came along, he was this handsome, charismatic older man who seemed like the answer to her prayers. I think she truly believed that he was going to rescue her and they would live happily ever after. Instead, she wound up in the same toxic relationship cycle her mother was trapped in.

The first time my mom divorced him was before Isaac was born. We were living in a mobile home on my grandma's property and my mom had enough of my dad getting high, so she kicked him out and filed for custody of my sister and me. Then one day, while my mom was at work, my dad went to my grandma's and told her he was taking me out to buy diapers. I was barely two years old so I have no memory of it. Apparently, instead of going to the store he took me down to the courthouse, filed a counterclaim against my mom, and got temporary custody of me. There's a part of me that still wants to believe he loved me so much he couldn't bear to be without me, but the truth is he was playing a game of tug of war with my mom. A few weeks later, out of desperation, my mom agreed to remarry him because it was the only way for her to get me back.

Me and my sister,
Victoria, circa 1995.

Maybe there was a part of her that wanted to believe he would change, but of course, he didn't. My dad couldn't hold down a steady job and she was constantly finding drugs on him. When she found out she was pregnant with his third child, my mom said she just sat on the floor and cried for hours. To make things worse, her doctor told her that the baby would have spina bifida, a birth defect where the spine doesn't form properly, and recommended that she terminate the pregnancy. Even though she didn't want to have another baby with my dad, she told the doctor, "I am not getting rid of my child. God gave me this life, and He is the only one who can take it away." It turned out the doctor was wrong about Isaac. When he was born, he only weighed three pounds. At first, they didn't think he was going to survive, but little by little he got stronger and he turned out to be a perfectly healthy baby. Meanwhile, my dad was more interested in getting high than meeting his son. When he finally got it together and brought me to the hospital to see my new baby brother, a bag of weed fell out of his pocket onto the floor right next to my mom's hospital bed.

That wasn't even the worst thing he did that week. A few days after my mom and Isaac were released from the hospital, we visited my great-grandmother in Jackson County so she could meet the new baby. As soon as we got there my mom told my sister and me to "go sit in the living room and don't move." We sat down on the floor in front of my great-grandma's television while the grownups sat on the couch chatting and watching the local news. When they got up to go talk in the kitchen, we knew not to get up and change the channel. If our mom told us to stay put that's what we did because we knew if we moved, we were in trouble. We didn't have much room to be children, so we sat quietly as we were told. Then, suddenly, my dad was on television. I remember seeing blue lights flashing on the screen, and my dad in handcuffs being put into the back of a police car.

"Mommy, Mommy!" I called out, "Daddy's on TV with the bad boys!"

I didn't really understand what he had done, but I knew that it must have been something really bad because she immediately started gathering up our things to leave. I heard her telling my aunt that she had to go find a bail bondsman because our no-good daddy got himself arrested for soliciting a prostitute. As she was loading us all into her Chevette, she was so blinded by anger that she didn't even see me standing there with my hand in the door. She slammed it so hard that my fingernail ended up turning black and falling off.

She told us later that when she went to arrange his bail, the bondsman looked at her in total disbelief and asked, "You're putting up the money to get this guy out of jail and you're the *wife*?" She was so humiliated that when she picked him up from jail, she made him kneel down on the floor in the backseat of her car so no one in town would see her driving him home. She wanted to leave him, but she had just had a baby. As long as he wasn't hurting her children, she felt like it was better if we didn't grow up in a broken home. To this day he swears the whole thing was a misunderstanding and the cop who arrested him was lying, but when we got older my mom took us to the town library to show us the records so we could read the truth for ourselves. According to the police report, he had approached an undercover police officer he thought was a prostitute and told her he only had ten dollars in his pocket so all he wanted was a blowjob.

A few months after Isaac was born, they split up for good. I remember thinking it was all my fault because they got into a huge fight about me right before my mom kicked him out. I had just started kindergarten and my mom was working as a janitor at CAMC Memorial Hospital in Charleston, so my dad was supposed to pick me up from the bus stop near my grandma's after school. When I got off the school bus there was no one there to meet me so I walked to my grandma's by myself. She wasn't home, but a cousin that was living with her at the time let me in. I was on my way to use the bathroom when I noticed his pocketknife sitting on a hutch in the corner of the dining room. I knew I wasn't supposed to play with knives, but I picked it up anyway and walked back towards the living room where my cousin was watching TV. For some reason, I decided it would be cool to open it behind my back. When I clicked the knife open, it was so sharp I didn't even feel the blade slice into my finger. "Look what I have," I said to my cousin. When I pulled my hand out from behind my back to show him the knife all I could see was blood, and there was a lot of it.

I don't really remember what happened next, but my dad was totally MIA so apparently my cousin called my mom at work. When he told her I had sliced my finger open, she got in touch with my grandmother who was working nearby. She rushed home to pick me up and drove me to meet my mom at the emergency room in Elkview. The cut was so deep I ended up with eight stitches in my finger and an ugly scar that never faded. My dad finally showed up hours later just as they were getting ready to discharge me. He started shouting at my mom right in the middle of the ER, demanding to know what the hell was going on. My mom was furious. She said a friend of hers told her that he was seen over on the west side of town buying dope when he should have been home to meet me after school. When she realized that people were staring at us, my mom said, "Gary, now is not the time nor the place. You put my child in danger. That is the last straw.

I am done. You need to go home, get your things, and get out. I don't care if you take everything I own, I just want you to get out and don't come back." Then she took us to a hotel for three days and didn't go home until she was sure he was gone.

As a five-year-old, all I knew was that I had done something bad and now my daddy was gone. After that, my mom was working all the time so she was never around anymore either. She had to work three jobs just to keep our heads above water. We were always being handed off to a family member or babysitters so she could work an extra shift at Subway or wait tables (on top of her job at the hospital). I was the oldest, so I instinctively stepped into the role of caretaker for my little brother and sister. Then my mom got remarried. All of a sudden, we had this stranger living in our house acting like he could tell us what to do. She met my stepdad, Lee, at the hospital where they were both working as janitors. Three months later, they were married. I think she grew to love him, but she was never *in* love with him. She was a twenty-three-year-old single mother of three and desperately wanted emotional and financial support. But, when this new man stepped into the picture, like he was in charge after I had been taking care of my siblings for so long, I became very combative. My attitude was, "I can take care of my brother and sister. You're not going to tell us what to do. We don't even know you."

Growing up, it seemed like my mom was angry all the time and she turned that anger on us. I believe she wanted to be better, but I don't think she even realized

Family portrait. From left to right: My mom, Victoria, me, Lee, Isaac.

how controlling and abusive she was. If we stepped out of line the least little bit, we got a smack across the mouth. If we didn't pick up our room the way she wanted it done, the punishment was to stand in a corner with our arms stretched out holding one of our stepdad's heavy boots in each hand. We would beg and cry to put the shoes down because our arms hurt so badly, but I remember she would make us stand there until she decided we were done. I think she carried all of that anger was because she never dealt with any of her pain. She felt abandoned, physically and emotionally, not only by my dad but by her own father who was never really in the picture. All that pain was always simmering just below the surface, and it would boil over and turn to rage whenever we didn't behave the way she wanted. It seemed like any feelings we ever expressed came with a punishment. So as I grew older, I shut down and became very anxious and fearful of everything.

After she remarried, we moved from my grandma's and lived in a couple of different rental homes around Boone County, where Lee grew up. We didn't see my dad much anymore. I want to believe that he tried at first, but my mom didn't make it easy for him. Whenever we would be upset as kids, wondering why we couldn't see our dad, she would say things like, "I'm here busting my butt off for you guys. Meanwhile, your dad's out there running the streets, doing drugs and God knows what else." Looking back, I understand why she was so hurt that we wanted him in our lives, though I wish she had tried harder to be less harsh with us to soften the blow. He'd call once or twice a year, if that, and every time he'd say, "I'm coming down to see you guys next weekend." We always believed him, but it never happened. Victoria and I would sit on the porch waiting for him for hours, but he never showed up—not one time.

We didn't really see him again until I was ten years old. He called out of the blue one day and said he was living down in Mingo County, about a hundred miles south, and he wanted us to come and stay with him. My mom didn't want us to have anything to do with our dad, but he still had court-ordered visitation rights. So she didn't have much of a choice. She reluctantly agreed to let us spend the weekend with him, as long as his mom, my

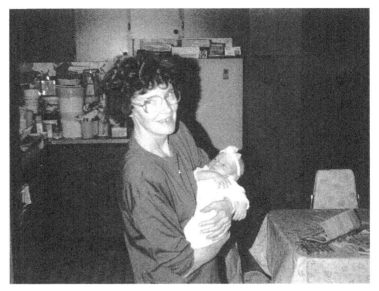

Me with Grandma Flo, my paternal grandmother who passed away in 2015. I still miss her to this day.

Grandma Flo, his sister, Laura, and her husband, Nile, agreed to check in on us. I was so excited we might as well have been going on a trip to Disney World. As I packed up my little bag and imagined the fun we were going to have with our daddy, all the hurt and disappointment from the times he never showed over the years just faded away. He swore to my mom he had gotten clean and was doing better, but of course, it was a lie. That weekend was nothing like the happy reunion I had been playing out in my mind.

He was living in a rundown trailer just outside of Kermit, a forgotten coal town near the border between West Virginia and Kentucky (which, ten years later, would become known as ground zero for the opioid epidemic).

It was basically just a shack on an isolated stretch of road along Route 52. There was nothing and no one for miles around, except for the massive 18-wheeler coal trucks that came flying past a couple of times an hour. My dad spent most of the first day in the back bedroom with a man in a wheelchair (who, I think, was his roommate) and some woman we'd never met, while Isaac, Victoria, and I sat on a dirty, beat-up old couch and watched cartoons on a crappy little television. Every so often random people would stop by and my dad would come out and talk to them. He looked nothing like the handsome preacher I remembered from when we were little. He'd been in a couple of car wrecks and suffered a stroke a few years earlier, so one side of his face was drooping. His hair was all greasy and he was missing a bunch of his teeth. He had allowed me to bring my little wiener dog, Leo, for the weekend, and we knew he was out of it because he kept calling Leo a cat and made me keep him in the bathtub.

The next morning, the woman he had been holing up with in the bedroom went out somewhere. We didn't know if she was his girlfriend, but we didn't like her. She was mean-looking, with stringy bleached yellow hair and acne scars all over her face. After she left, my dad finally came out of the bedroom and said, "If y'all want me to be able to come and pick you up more often, you need to go outside and help me collect as many cans as you can." I mean, what kid doesn't want to spend a Saturday morning picking up trash by the side of the road for their dad? We left Isaac inside watching TV. Then Victoria and I went out front and starting gathering up all the empty beer and soda cans we could find around the trailer. We put them into a little pile by the fire pit. For a while he was standing out there, telling us where we should look, but eventually, he lost interest. Before he disappeared back inside the trailer, he pointed to the field across the road and told me to make sure we got all the cans over there too. I knew he wanted to trade them in for money, so I was determined to collect as many as I could find. I crossed the road and picked through the knee-high grass looking for cans until my arms were full. I felt I had a pretty good haul. I couldn't wait for my dad to tell me how proud he was of me.

That's when the mean-looking girlfriend came back. She pulled up in her car, took one look at me standing in the field with my arms full of dirty, dented cans and hollered, "Gary! Get out here! Leah's over there playing on the other side of the road." My dad came to the door, "Leah!" he shouted. "Get your ass back over here, right now!" I couldn't understand why I was in trouble when he had just told me not ten minutes before to go and get all these cans, but I did what I was told and ran back. As I was crossing, an 18-wheeler came barreling down the road. I panicked and started running as fast as I could towards the trailer. It was so close when it flew past me that I could feel the vibrations on my back. Just as I reached the other side of the road I tripped, and all my cans went flying all over the place.

Next thing I knew, my dad had scooped me up off the ground and was carrying me over his arm back towards the trailer. For a second I thought he was going to comfort me, but then he grabbed a switch from the pile of wood next to the fire pit, pulled down my pants, and started whipping me with it. As I was screaming and crying, trying to get away, I heard the girlfriend say, "You better hold still, honey, or it's gonna hurt worse." Then Victoria jumped up on our dad's back and started pounding him with her little fists. "Leave her alone!" she shouted. "It's your fault. You told her. You told her to do it!" He shook her off like a rag doll and kept whipping me.

That wasn't the first time he lost his temper and beat me like that. Back when my mom was pregnant with Isaac, we went to visit my Grandpa Messer in Columbus, Ohio. I remember being downstairs in the basement with my dad's half-sister, Jennifer, who was the favorite child. I was goofing around and shot water at her through my teeth. She yelled at me and then my dad came down, grabbed me by the arm, and dragged me outside. The switch he grabbed to whip me with must have had thorns because I could feel them tearing into my skin as he was smacking my legs with it.

This time, when he finally put me down, Victoria and I immediately took off and hid. I don't know how much time passed, but at some point, he started building a fire. We could see that he was burning something from where we were hiding, maybe some of the trash that was all over the property. Then he started cutting open the cans we had collected. We heard him swear and I realized that he had cut himself. I knew he had been bad to me, but I couldn't help feeling sorry for him. I went into the trailer, found some supplies to clean and bandage up the cut, and then sat down by the fire next to him. I could tell he was totally strung out. As I was cleaning his cut, he looked at me and said with such sadness, "You know I love you, Leah."

I don't remember if we called my Aunt Laura because we were scared, or if they just stopped by to check in on us, but when she and Niles came by with my Grandma Flo the next morning I just burst into tears. I didn't know what else to say, so I told them, "He keeps saying my dog is a cat and that he is pooping and peeing everywhere, but it's not true." When Victoria told them that he had beat me after I almost got hit by a coal truck, they called our mom and said she better come get us right away. She must have flown down there at a hundred miles an hour because by the time they got us packed up and out of the house she had pulled up to the trailer and told us to get in the car.

That's when all hell broke loose. My dad came out and started hollering at my mom that she couldn't take his kids. We were sitting in the backseat of my mom's car, crying and holding onto each other. When he started banging on the window my Grandma Flo tried to tell him to just let us go, but he just got in her face and told her to mind her fucking business. Then my mom started shouting that he needed to respect his mother. He was so angry and aggressive that my aunt and uncle had to get between him and my grandma. As we were driving off I could hear my dad screaming, "You know that I love you, Leah! You know that I love you!"

We didn't see him again for another three years.

Chapter Two:

A TREE WITHOUT ROOTS CAN'T GROW

During my entire childhood, I don't think we ever lived in any one place for much longer than a year. Any time my mom got into a confrontation or encountered adversity, her instinct was to just pull up stakes and move on. It seemed like she was always running from something and searching for a fresh start. But no matter, where we went or how many times we started over in a new town (or even a new state), it was always the same. By the time we had unpacked and settled in somewhere, it was never long before something would trigger her impulse to run and we'd be boxing it all up again for the next move. The core of your happiness has to come from within—otherwise, it won't matter how far you run, the unhappiness is going to follow you wherever you go.

Dressed up as Barbie for Halloween in kindergarten.

My grandma's house in Clay County, West Virginia, was the most consistent address we had. She owned a three-story home on around a hundred acres of land in Bomont, way out in the countryside. My mom kept a single-wide trailer home on the property behind the house, and we lived there on and off throughout my childhood. But most of the time we were bouncing back and forth from different low-income apartments or rental homes all over West Virginia, and as far as North Carolina and Columbus, Ohio. For me, the consequence of all that moving around was that I never felt like I fit in anywhere because we were never in one place long enough for me to set down roots. Not only was I unsure of myself socially, it got to the point where I always felt confused in class

First grade.

because we would learn one thing at one school and then go to another school. At the new school, what they were working on would be completely different—different chapter, different subject, different everything. Sadly, I had no idea moving around that much wasn't normal. I just thought there was something wrong with *me*.

For most of my childhood, and even through high school, the only constant friendship I had in my chaotic life was with my best friend, Kayla Roush. I first met Kayla in second grade at H.E. White Elementary School, just down the road from my grandma's house. At first, we had a catty little fight about another girl in our class, but we quickly realized she was playing us against each other. From that moment on, we were inseparable. Kayla and

I instinctively gravitated towards one another because we both understood what it was like to live in a family with so much toxic dysfunction. Her father was an abusive alcoholic and her mother was always working to make ends meet, so Kayla, being the second oldest of five, became the caretaker for her younger siblings.

Kayla was the only person outside of my family that I felt like I could trust enough to truly be myself around. We had the same sense of humor, the same taste in clothes, the same unhappy home lives, and the same need to take care of everyone but ourselves. We even looked so much alike that people often mistook us for twins, which we loved—we would always beg my grandma to take us shopping at the mall so we could buy matching outfits to wear to school. When my mom decided, on the spur of the moment, to move to Walkertown, North Carolina, before the end of the school year I was heartbroken. We were there for a little less than a year. I can still remember the feeling of excitement when a card from Kayla would come for me in the mail, or I when I got to hear her voice on a message that she had left on our answering machine. When we moved back to my grandma's a year later, I got to go back to school at H.E. White with Kayla again. It was like a celebration. We picked up right where we left off and I knew we would be best friends forever. We moved back to North Carolina a second time in my fifth-grade year and it was tough, but by then we were old enough to write letters back and forth and talk on the phone for hours. We were the only support system we had in the

Me and Kayla just before we moved to North Carolina in my fifth-grade year.

chaos of our home lives and we kept each other's heads above water.

By the time I started middle school, we had moved back to West Virginia for good, but my mom's pattern of uprooting us every few months didn't stop. Between sixth and seventh grade I went to three different schools and lived in four or five different homes in almost as many towns. We moved into the main house on my grandma's property the summer before sixth grade, so I started that school year with Kayla at Clay County Middle School. Like most eleven-year-olds, I desperately wanted to fit in and make friends. At that point in my life, I wasn't super outgoing—but I wanted to be. Deep down I had this big, fun-loving personality, but I was so boxed in and insecure that I had to know you and trust you to be myself. Even after I started to make friends, one of the biggest issues that I struggled with in middle school (and then even into high school) was that they never wanted to come over and hang out or have sleepovers at my house because they didn't feel comfortable around my mom. She always came off as angry and too strict. I would have friends come over once and then after that, if I invited them over again, they always said, "Let's go to my house because your mom's mean and she won't let us do anything."

All the kids I was hanging out with were involved in athletics and after-school activities. I wanted to fit in, play sports, and be part of a team like all my other friends, but I didn't have that kind of support at home. I had no one to give me the direction I needed to go where I wanted in life, so I was just kind of lost. I had played a little basketball in elementary school when I went to H.E. White, so I decided to try out for the team at Clay. I was terrible. Even though I was naturally athletic, no one had ever practiced with me at home or taught me basic skills like how to dribble and pass. When that didn't work out, I tried out for the cheer team. I was so excited and proud of myself when I made the cut, but I was way behind the other girls on the team who had all been taking gymnastics classes and doing one-on-one private sessions for years. I remember a couple of them laughing and making fun of me at practice because I didn't have my back handspring. But I knew not to ask my mom for lessons. The only reason she had even agreed to let me be on the cheer team in the first place was because the school had a bus that took us home every day after practice. If she had to pick me up, pay extra money, or if it interfered with her work schedule, there was no way it was happening.

However embarrassed as I was about my tumbling skills, it was nothing compared to when my mom decided it would be fun to experiment with my hair. By the time she was done putting in all the chemicals to bleach and perm my hair, it was such a fried mess that I looked like I had a frizzy banana on my head. But my mom actually thought it looked great, so I just went along with it because I was never able to speak up for myself, especially at home. Going to school the next day was totally humiliating; everyone was asking me what the heck I did to my hair and laughing at me behind my back. I was already insecure about the gap in my teeth, but now I hated everything about how I looked. I desperately wanted braces, but we couldn't afford them (and Medicaid would only pay for them if they were medically necessary). Since I couldn't do anything about my hair, except wait for it to grow out, I decided to try and fix my teeth myself. I remember sneaking into the bathroom with a pair of pliers every night while I was getting ready for bed and trying to use them to force my teeth closer together.

After that, I started to develop intense anxiety about going to school. I would hide under my bed every morning and beg my mom to let me stay home. Most of the time she would just let me skip. The truth is, it made her life easier when I stayed home from school because I would do chores, help with the housework, and be around to help take care of my brother and sister. My mom had dropped out after eighth grade. The importance of an education was never expressed to her growing up, so school was never really a priority for her. We got in trouble if we didn't bring home good grades, but it wasn't because she wanted us to get into a good college. In her mind, school was just someplace you went until you were old enough to get a real job and settle down with a family.

The only people I had in my life who ever encouraged me to be a child were my mom's brother, Danny, and his wife, Misty. They had bought the property next to my grandma's, and they were living next door in a modular home at the time. They had a completely different parenting style. I used to walk over and visit with them. They would try to get me to play like a young child should without any responsibility. They didn't agree with a lot of my mom's parenting choices and wished for me to be the child that I was. But that was all I had ever known. I had been watching my brother and sister from the time I was in kindergarten, so I felt protecting them was my responsibility.

I ended up having to switch schools again because my mom got into a huge fight with Misty over the way she was parenting us. On one of the days my mom let me stay home from school, she called from work and told me I had to go down to H. E. White to pick up Isaac (who was in first grade at the time) because they were sending him home with a fever. The school was about a mile from my grandma's house and I would have to walk down there and then walk back with Isaac, but I was used to caring for my siblings so I didn't really think much of it. But when Isaac's teacher, Miss Varney, found out my mom was sending me to pick him up she immediately called Misty. Bomont is a town with a population of four hundred people. Everybody knows everybody. Miss Varney had grown up with my mom, aunt, and uncle. They had actually all gone to school together as kids. So she had no problem calling up Misty and telling her that it was absolutely unacceptable for my mom to send a child to pick up another child who was sick with a fever.

Misty ended up going down to the school to get Isaac herself. When my mom found out she was pissed. She got into it with my aunt, and then my grandma got involved. It turned into a big family feud because they were calling her out for putting too much responsibility on me. My mom did not like anyone interfering or questioning her authority over her kids, so she stopped speaking to all of them. She just cut them out of our lives completely. We moved out of my grandma's and into a rental out on Frame Road in Elkview. It was only in the next county over, but it was a different school district. I begged my mom to not make me transfer because I had already been in so many schools, but we were now forty miles from Clay, so my mom had to drive fifteen minutes to the county line to drop me off at the nearest school bus stop. She did that for maybe a week or two, but it was just too much for her to make that drive every morning. So she pulled me out of Clay.

Halfway through the school year I had to leave my best friend, quit the cheer team, and start over at Elkview Middle School. I was totally miserable. I hated being at yet another new school where I didn't know anyone and no one knew me. Every morning I woke up with this feeling of dread in the pit of my stomach. The sad thing is, I actually liked school. I loved learning new things and I craved the structure—which I didn't have at home. I hated always being the new kid. Every time I had to start over it chipped away at my self-esteem, and I retreated into myself a little bit more.

I was too young to understand that never having any kind of solid foundation under my feet was the real reason I didn't want to go to school. I was never able to express my feelings to my mom because I was afraid I'd be accused of back talking or questioning her parenting and get into trouble. Punishments tended to be brutal at times too—we were spanked, smacked, and paddled. We never really knew how a punishment was going to go down, or even how my mom would react to simply expressing how we felt. But, as harsh as she could be, my mom was also very manipulative. When I cried about school or because I missed my grandma, she would cuddle me up and say, "I'm here for you, baby. I'm always here for you." She knew exactly how to make us feel guilty, so we never spoke up for ourselves or rebelled against the choices she made that impacted us negatively. It was easier to just shut down and beg not to go to school.

A few weeks after I started at Elkview, my English teacher humiliated me in front of the whole class. In Ms. Brown's class, the minute she turned her back everyone would start fooling around. Kids liked her class because she had so little control you could get away with goofing off, and no one respected her because she would lose her temper and throw kids out of her classroom over the most ridiculous things. I rarely ever spoke in any of my classes or did anything to draw attention to myself. I was already painfully shy and self-conscious, so when Ms. Brown scolded me in front of all the other kids because I didn't have a pencil, it was my worst nightmare. I could feel everyone's eyes on me and heard a couple of kids laughing under their breath. I was so embarrassed that, instead of holding my tongue, I decided to give her attitude because I was humiliated. I thought I was standing up for myself. Instead, it got me thrown out of the classroom and I had to spend the rest of the period standing out in the hallway.

After that, I started getting sick all the time. I don't know if it was all the stress breaking down my immune system or if I was just prone, but I got strep throat so many times that I barely went to school the rest of the year. I'd come down with a sore throat and a fever and then be out for weeks at a time. I never settled in or started to feel comfortable at Elkview because I never got the chance to establish any friendships before my mom was on the move again. She and my stepfather got into an argument with the people we were renting the house from, so they uprooted us again and we moved to Charleston.

At this point, I had come down with strep so many times that I couldn't even start seventh grade at South Charleston Middle School right away because I had to get my tonsils and adenoids taken out. I don't remember much about the surgery, except that in the car on the way home from the hospital after it was over, my mom handed me a journal my grandma had left for me. She must have tried to see me after the surgery, but my mom wouldn't let her because she was still angry about the fight. The journal was covered in pretty flowers. Inside there was a letter from my grandma telling me how much she loved me and missed me, and that she hoped I would use it to write down all my hopes and dreams. The letter was sweet and loving, but underneath there was such sadness. Not being allowed to see our grandma was so heartbreaking. All our lives she had taken care of us whenever my mom was working; she cooked for us, took us shopping for school clothes, and was one of the only consistent sources of love we had ever known. Not allowing her to see her grandkids was probably the worst thing that my mom could do to her. What I don't think she realized was that she was punishing *us* too. It sent a message to us that nothing in our lives—not even family—was permanent. She ended up making up with my grandma a month or two later, but the fact that we watched our mom repeatedly cut people out of her life so easily would have a lasting impact on all three of us.

Meanwhile, I had been out of school and hanging out by myself at home for so long that after I recovered from the surgery, I was actually looking forward to going back and being around other kids my age. Charleston is less than twenty miles from Elkview, but it might as well have been on another planet. For most of my life, we had lived in small, rural towns with populations that barely topped out at a thousand people. Now, all of a sudden, we were living in the capital of West Virginia, which to me seemed like this big, fast-paced city. The kids at South Charleston Middle School were totally different from the kids I had met at my previous schools. The way they dressed was different, the way they acted was different, even the way they talked was different. At all the schools I had been to before nobody thought twice if you wore raggedy hand-me-downs and scuffed up shoes, but at South Charleston all the kids were into expensive sneakers, designer jeans, and cool clothes—which, of course, I didn't have. I remember showing up on that first day, wearing a dingy T-shirt, no-name jeans, and bargain store shoes. I felt like I looked like a country mouse in the big city. Once again, I was the new kid who was out of step with everyone around me, but I was determined to stick it out and fit in because being in a big city with no friends and no family was so lonely and isolating.

Between all the school I had missed from the end of sixth grade to the beginning of seventh and how far ahead the curriculum was at this new school, I was so far behind in all of my classes it seemed like I would never catch up. I remember sitting in math class, looking at the equations the teacher had put up on the chalkboard, and feeling totally lost, like she was writing in some kind of alien language. It was the same thing in all my classes. I should have raised my hand or gone to speak to my teachers after class, but I was too afraid to ask for help. I just kept my head down and tried not to draw any attention to myself.

Socially, things were a little better than at my last school—at least, at first. I hit it off almost immediately with a girl named Katy who sat next to me in homeroom. She was sweet and funny, and for the first time since I had started middle school, I began to relax and feel like I could be myself. I ended up being absorbed into her circle of friends. We all got along great and they were fun to hang out with, but at the same time, these girls had known each other forever. So there was a part of me that always felt like I was a little on the outside; like they had a secret language or were all in on some inside joke that I just didn't get. I had a crush on this cute boy in our friend group named Jonathan. Katy liked his best friend, so the four of us went on a couple of double dates to the movies.

South Charleston was much more ethnically diverse than Clay or Elkview, so a lot of my new friends were Black and Hispanic. The difference in the color of our skin wasn't something that I was even really aware of until my grandfather refused to come to my birthday party because my "Black boyfriend" was going to be there. That was the first time I saw a glimpse of the cruel man who was full of hate that my mother had grown up with, instead of the loving grandfather I had always known.

Despite how hurt I was by my grandfather's racist boycott of my thirteenth birthday party, things were actually going well for me in South Charleston. I had friends, a cute boyfriend, and I was finally starting to feel like I had some solid ground under my feet—which were now decked out in my first pair of Nike high tops, thanks to Jonathan who gave them to me as a present for my birthday. Then one day, I was walking from second period to my next class and a girl I didn't even know jumped me. I remember stepping through the set of double doors that led from the hallway into the stairwell. My arms were full of books because we only had four minutes between classes and we weren't allowed to go back to our lockers until lunch. The girl must have snuck back to her locker before the end of second period and put all her books away because she was waiting for me (with her arms free) behind one of the doors. I was getting ready to go down the stairs when she came out from what seemed like nowhere and sucker-punched me right in the face.

I've never been a fighter, but I was tougher than I looked. Back when I was in fifth grade with Kayla, we used to be part of what I can only describe as an elementary school Fight Club. In the schoolyard at H.E. White, there was this log cabin-like structure that was completely empty inside. Kids used it as a kind of clubhouse, and every day at recess there would be these prearranged fights. It was totally under the radar, but also highly organized. There was a kid who would referee the fight and brackets where you could bet on who would win. All I ever wanted was to fit in, so of course, I ended up getting pulled into a couple of fights. You'd be down on the ground wrestling, pulling hair, punching and kicking each other, doing whatever you had to do to stay in the fight until one of you finally gave in. I was actually undefeated, and then on my third or fourth fight, the girl I was up against got hurt and we all got in trouble. I tackled her and took her down, but as she was squirming around on the ground, she hit her kneecap on the wooden wall of the cabin and it split open. Suddenly, there was blood all over her knee and all the kids that had been watching and cheering us on instantly scattered—that was the end of my junior wrestling career.

I was little, but I knew how to defend myself, so when that girl attacked me in the stairwell, I remember taking a second to process the pain and then I instinctively dropped all my books and started fighting back. As we were punching and kicking each other, I was vaguely aware that kids from all over the school had come running to watch and had begun chanting, "Fight! Fight! Fight!" The next thing I remember was a couple of teachers pulling us apart and both of us being sent to the principal's office. They called my mom and we both ended up getting suspended for three days, even though I was just defending myself. To this day, I have no idea why she attacked me.

Me, Victoria, and Isaac—just before we moved back to West Virginia from North Carolina.

That was it. I shut down completely. Whatever confidence I had gained over the past few months completely evaporated, and it was replaced by a familiar, paralyzing sense of dread about going to school. I begged my mom, "Please, don't make me go back there. I don't want to go. Please, homeschool me. I'll do all my work from home. I'll do anything; just don't make me go back there." We ended up moving again pretty much right after the fight anyway because the lease was up on the place we were renting and my mom found a cheaper apartment in Dunbar. We had moved less than five miles from South Charleston, but Dunbar was in a different school district, which meant that I would have to start over again at another new school. Isaac and Victoria finished the year at Dunbar Intermediate School, but I was done. I had been to three schools in less than two years, and it hadn't gone well for me at any of them.

That was the end of middle school for me. My mom let me stay home for the rest of that year and for all of eighth grade. It was convenient for her because I was around to help with chores and take care of my brother and sister while she and my stepdad were at work, but it's not like she put me in any kind of homeschool program. I don't remember reading a single book or filling out any worksheets that year. At some point, I took a test that allowed me to technically pass eighth grade, but I didn't step foot inside a classroom again until high school.

Chapter Three:

YES GIRL

My entire life I have struggled with saying no. The worst mistakes I've made were because I didn't know how to say no in situations that made me feel bad about myself. This was a pattern that began in my childhood because I felt like I wasn't allowed to speak up for myself at home. I was always afraid my mom would get angry and withhold her love if I wasn't a good girl. Unfortunately, I carried this distorted sense of what it meant to be loved out into the world with me, and "yes" became my default whenever I wanted someone to like me. I allowed things to happen to me that I didn't want because in my mind the most important thing was to be liked—more important even than liking myself.

The first time I can remember not being able to say no to something I didn't want was when I was about five or six years old. This was after my parents split up, but before my mom met my stepfather. She was working at the hospital in Charleston, and my grandma couldn't always watch us, so she would drop us off with a family that lived in Clendenin on her way to work. They were pretty well known in the community and they had three older children. The youngest daughter was kind of a bully (who later on would pick on Victoria in school), so we didn't really like playing with her. We never saw the oldest daughter because she was always in her bedroom. The mom was mean and used to scold us, but the middle daughter, who was about fourteen or fifteen, used to help her babysit us. I thought she was the coolest person I had ever met. She was kind of a tomboy and she would invent all these really fun games for us to play. My favorite was when we would pretend to be different characters from Xena Warrior Princess and run around the backyard with toy swords. Sometimes she would chase me and try to kiss me, and I would have to run away and hide. I really wanted her to like me, but at the same time, she made me feel weird and uncomfortable.

Then, she started lying down with me at naptime. She would put on a movie and as soon as her mother left the room, she would kiss my neck and touch me where no one should ever touch a child. I didn't like what she was doing. It felt wrong, but she was the only one in that house that was nice to us. I was afraid that if I told her to stop, she wouldn't want to hang out and play games anymore. This went on for at least six months. Every morning, I'd beg my mom not to take me there. She'd get annoyed, so I'd cry my eyes out in the car the whole way. And then it would happen all over again. I never told my mom what she was doing to me and it never occurred to her that I wasn't just being difficult.

Eventually, it stopped because we moved to North Carolina, but I never told anyone because I felt so ashamed—like I had done something wrong. I stuffed the memory down so deep it was almost as if it never happened. Except that it did, and it became another loose stone in the foundation of my self-worth. It took a long time for me to find my voice because I didn't know how to love myself enough to say no. It wasn't until I had daughters of my own that I began to realize I had to learn to value myself so they would know, without hesitation, when to speak up for themselves.

After we moved to Dunbar, I lost contact with Katy and Jonathan. My eighteen-year-old cousin was living with us, so I spent most of my days babysitting her two-year-old while she was working at McDonald's, doing chores around the house, and watching cartoons on TV. At an age when most kids are just beginning to figure out who they are and where they fit in, my life narrowed to the point where I barely left the house or saw anyone outside my family. I wasn't going to school so I wasn't learning anything. I wasn't interacting with other kids my age and I wasn't growing emotionally. It was the loneliest year of my life.

By the winter of what should have been my eighth-grade year, I was so sick of being stuck in the house that when my mom arranged for me to go to Florida for a week with my stepfather, I was actually excited. Lee and

From left to right: Victoria, me, Isaac, and Mom.

I had never gotten along. We butted heads right from the beginning. I was combative because I resented him for stepping in and thinking he had the right to tell us what to do, and he was harsh with us because he thought his role as our stepfather was to lay down the law. Whenever there was a conflict, it felt like he always wanted my mom to choose between him and us. He loved her, but we came with the package, and I think he just had no idea what he was getting into when he married a woman with three kids.

My disapproval turned to hatred when I was around twelve years old after he spanked me for rolling my eyes at him. We were living in the same house as my aunt and uncle, and in front of everybody, he picked me up by one arm and smacked me three times on my backside so hard that hot tears of pain and humiliation instantly stung my eyes. I remember looking over at my mom and asking, "How can you let him do that do me?" I wanted her to defend me. I wanted her to tell Lee to never lay a hand on her child again. I wanted her to take *my* side for once, but she didn't say a word. She just sat there and let it happen. Then, as though to prove that he had won and was in control, he spanked me again. That night I cried myself to sleep, vowing I would *never* forgive him for hitting me.

By the time I was thirteen, we had settled into something that resembled a truce. I still didn't really want anything to do with him, but as I got older, I was able to recognize that he provided for us and was a faithful husband to my mom—which I figured had to count for something. Mostly, I was just resigned to the reality that he wasn't going anywhere, which at the very least was good for my mom. When she told me that Lee was taking me with him to Florida, I definitely had mixed feelings about the trip. On the one hand, I had never been to Florida and I was so excited to see the ocean and sit on the beach. On the other, our relationship was so awkward that I couldn't imagine spending a whole week with Lee on my own.

It turned out we didn't have to spend much time together anyway. Lee was in the process of getting his nursing license and had been hired to go down to Florida to help take care of a family friend who was recovering from a major surgery. The reason I had been invited on the trip wasn't so that he and I could have some kind of stepfather-stepdaughter bonding experience, it was so that

With Lee, on our trip to Ocala, FL.

their teenage son would have someone he could hang out with while they were down there. I had actually known Josh my whole life. Our moms were close friends, so we had played together a lot when we were little. My mom used to drop us off at their house while she was working and we'd play tag or cops and robbers. He was five years older than me, so I had always thought of him as an annoying older cousin, but now that I was thirteen and he was eighteen I suddenly saw him in a whole new light. All of a sudden, he was this cute high school senior who was so tall, tan, and muscular that he looked like he had stepped right out of the pages of a J. Crew catalog.

We were all staying in a cabin in Ocala, near Silver Springs State Park, and during the day Lee or Josh's mom would drop us off at different activities. On the first day, we went to Alexander Springs, but it ended up being too cold to swim so we didn't do much. We were both kind of bored and didn't really have much to say to each other. Then at some point, Josh asked me if I had ever been kayaking. When I told him that I hadn't, he said, "Are you, kidding? I can't believe you've never been. It's so much fun. We should totally go." So the next day Lee dropped us off at the entrance to Silver Springs and we rented a couple of kayaks.

For some reason, we thought it would be fun to paddle out to where the glass-bottom boats were doing alligator tours—which was a stupid idea to begin with, given that the only thing between us and the gators would be the thin plastic of our bright orange rental kayaks. It ended up being a super windy day (we found out later it was actually some kind of a record for Central Florida). On the way out, I was able to keep up with Josh because it was easy to paddle when we had the wind at our backs, but it was harder than hell once we realized how far out we were and tried to turn around to head back to the entrance. Josh probably would have been fine on his own, but I got stuck because I didn't have the strength in my skinny thirteen-year-old arms to paddle against thirty-five mile-per-hour winds. I struggled for a while without making any progress. Then Josh came up with the idea of taking out the string from the waistband of his swim trunks and using it to tie our kayaks together so he could tow me back to the entrance. The wind was so strong that after about twenty minutes we still weren't getting anywhere. At this point, I was definitely starting to panic. Eventually, we had no choice but to paddle to the nearest embankment, where there was sandbar so we could get out and drag our kayaks to shore.

I was relieved to finally be out of the water and on (semi) dry land, but we were still at least a mile from the entrance. There was no path and we were in straight-up swampland, so there were definitely snakes and gators out there. All we could do was skirt the edge of the river, and a bunch of times we had to wade through knee-deep water just to keep moving forward. I could barely manage carrying our paddles on my own, so Josh ended up having to haul both kayaks on his back the whole way. By the time we finally made it back to the entrance, we were both exhausted and completely sunburnt from being stuck out on the water for so long—but it was the most thrilling adventure I had ever had. That night Josh asked me to go for a walk with him so he could smoke some weed and get high, and I just remember thinking that I was totally, head over heels in love.

When we got back home to West Virginia, Josh and I started chatting and flirting a little bit on AOL Instant Messenger. I was so naive I actually thought this meant we were in a relationship. It didn't help that I felt like my mom and his mom were encouraging me. I remember hearing them talk about how he liked me too and how fun it would be if they were grandmothers together. It didn't take much for me to become absolutely convinced that this was the boy I was going to marry. Josh was eighteen and about to graduate from high school, and I was a thirteen-year-old who hadn't been to school in almost a

Following the teen mom cycle: My mom was sixteen when she had me, one year younger than I was when I got pregnant.

year. I'm not sure the age difference seemed as big a deal to them as it should have. There's a small-town mentality that comes into play, and the truth is, it wasn't uncommon where I grew up for girls to get married and start having kids at a very young age.

My mom had dropped out of school at thirteen to help her mother out at home, and then she had me just a few years after that. She married my father (who she loved, but was an emotionally unavailable drug addict) to escape the unhappiness of living with an abusive stepfather. She married Lee (who she didn't love, but was devoted to her) to escape the uncertainty of struggling to get by as a single mother. I think she did want better for me, but she was so trapped in those toxic relationship cycles that she wasn't capable of guiding me out of the dysfunction.

In her mind, the best I could do was to settle down with a cute boy and start a family of my own. Meanwhile, she wasn't happy or fulfilled in her own life because she had made major life choices for all the wrong reasons.

By the time I was thirteen she had just turned thirty, and I think she started to feel like she had been missing out on something. She was lonely in her marriage so she joined a Yahoo group where you could meet people, video chat, and sign up for karaoke contests. Her chat name was "wantgiveget" and she developed a community of online friends through the group. She created this whole other life and persona for herself online, and eventually, she started having flirtations with men on the side. She wasn't even secretive about it. By then, her boundaries with me had gotten very blurry when it came to men. She would talk to me about these flirtations and let me read the messages they were sending to each other. At the time, it seemed totally normal—and I didn't like Lee anyway, so it wasn't like I was going to tell him what she was doing—but looking back it seems so clear to me now how her behavior was informing my understanding of what it meant to be in a relationship. I was watching my mom flirt with men online, and then emulating that with a boy who was way too old for me.

The first time I ever smoked pot was with Josh. We had been chatting on AIM and it was fun and flirty. I was like, "Oh, my gosh, he *definitely* likes me." He was so cute and (in my mind at least) we started dating. When he asked me if I wanted to go out joyriding with him and his buddies, I was so excited. Until I got in the car and realized Josh's

ex-girlfriend was driving and I'd be hanging out with her all night too. I knew they had slept together and it made me feel insecure and jealous. Looking back, I wonder just how many other girls he was "dating," but at the time I definitely thought *I* was the only one. They were all passing around a joint and getting high. I had always been very anti-drugs because of my dad, but when they passed it to me, I felt like I couldn't say no or they would all look at me like I was just a little kid. I had never tried pot before and had no interest in doing it again, but that one time was enough to get me in huge trouble.

A couple of days later my mom found a bag of weed on top of our refrigerator. I'm pretty sure it belonged to my cousin (because it definitely wasn't mine), but my mom was so furious that she actually went out and bought an over-the-counter drug testing kit. Then she stood in the bathroom with me and watched while I peed in the cup. When I tested positive for marijuana she totally flipped out. I remember she grabbed me up by my shirt and threw me in my room. I wanted to tell her that I had only done it because I felt pressured by these older kids I was hanging out with, but she was so angry that I couldn't find the words. I wish she had sat me down and tried to talk to me about what had happened. I wish that she had chosen to parent me instead of punish me. I wish that she had tried to help me understand that I didn't have to say yes to things I wasn't ready for just to get a boy to like me. If she had, maybe she could have prevented what happened next.

A couple of weeks later, my mom and Lee took Isaac and Victoria to visit my grandmother. I wanted to hang out with Josh, but I was still grounded. Whenever my mom and Lee went out for the night, my cousin would always call her boyfriend and they would disappear into her bedroom. I decided to tell my mom that I wasn't feeling well so she would let me stay home. As soon as they all pulled out in the car, I messaged Josh on AIM and invited him over. Our place in Dunbar was a forty-five-minute drive from Bomont, which meant they would be out for a couple of hours at least. Josh didn't have a car, but he only lived a few miles up the road, so he could walk to my house and we'd still have at least an hour before they got home. I remember feeling so grown up about having a "date" with Josh while my mom was out of the house. I was so blown away by him. When he kissed me, it was even better than I had imagined it would be. I had this romantic (and totally delusional) fantasy going on in my head that we were falling in love. After our adventure on the kayaks in Silver Springs, it felt like we had all this history. It was like we were meant to be. We were definitely going to get married and live happily ever after.

The next thing I knew we were upstairs in my bedroom and Josh was on top of me. I remember him fumbling around with the condom because he was trying to hurry before my mom came back. Then he took my virginity so fast I didn't even have time to process what was happening before it was already over. It hurt so much when he pushed inside me, I couldn't help crying. I wanted to be cool about it, but I really didn't even fully comprehend what we just had just done. As soon as it was over, I started to panic because there was so much blood and I was terrified my mom would see the stains on my sheets. Josh was worried we were going to get caught, so I called my mom and it turned out they were already in the car on the way home. After I got off the phone with my mom, Josh jumped off my bed, pulled on his jeans, and left.

That was my first time being intimate—my first *anything*. I remember lying on my bed after he left, feeling used and worthless. I had never even kissed a boy before, but I wanted him to like me so I was afraid to say no. When my mom got home ten minutes later, she knocked on my bedroom door and said, "You're not going to believe who we saw walking up the road when we stopped in at the gas station...Josh! Such a nice boy!"

After that night, it happened again a few more times. I would go over to Josh's house and, if no one was home, we would go straight up to his bedroom. If his mom was home, we would watch TV for a little bit and then go up to his bedroom. I think somewhere deep down I could feel him pulling away and losing interest, but I wanted so desperately to believe in the fantasy I had created that I kept saying yes, even though it always left me feeling empty inside.

Chapter Four:

I JUST WANT SOMEBODY TO LOVE ME

It took me a long time to learn the difference between *being* loved and *feeling* loved. The problem is that you don't always feel loved when you are, and you can convince yourself that you feel loved when you aren't. *Being* loved is unconditional. It's the kind of love I have for my daughters. The kind of love you need to have for yourself in order to be a whole person. *Feeling* loved can be an illusion you create in your own heart to fill the emptiness. If you don't love yourself, being loved will never feel like enough. You wind up hungering for the illusion and pushing away the real thing.

In the middle of that emotional rollercoaster with Josh, my dad called out of the blue and said he wanted to see us. He was living down in Yulee, Florida, in a trailer behind his father's second home. My Grandpa Messer owned a business in Columbus and lived there most of the year, but he was driving down to Florida with my Grandma Caroline (his second wife). They offered to pick me, my brother, and my sister up on the way so we could have a visit with our dad. My mom wasn't crazy about the idea (to say the least), but there wasn't much she could do about it. He still had court-mandated visitation rights he could fall back on whenever he decided to get it together long enough to resurface in our lives.

We hadn't seen him for a good long while, not since he had whooped me for crossing the road, but despite all he'd done, we still hungered to see our dad. We didn't know what to expect when we got down there, but he actually seemed to be doing pretty well. His trailer wasn't dirty. He wasn't living with a bunch of random people. He seemed just like a normal single guy living on his own. The first couple of days he took us out and we did fun stuff. We drove out to some local cold springs and went tubing. We saw a snake, and I freaked out because ever since we got stuck out on those kayaks I have been *terrified* of snakes. Those first few days were like the happy family vacation we never had with our dad but always wanted. We went to a big Messer family barbecue and played with cousins we hadn't seen for years. It was the happiest we had been with our dad since before he and our mom split up.

By day four, it started getting bad again. He stopped taking us out to do fun things and we just hung around the house all day. Victoria and I would play with the neighbor's kid or go for walks on this dirt road behind the property while our dad sat on the couch watching TV and drinking beer. He was obsessed with the koozies that kept your cans cold. At one point, I told him I had a headache, and instead of aspirin, he gave me a Soma. I didn't know that it was a muscle relaxer; all I knew was that it made me feel drowsy and weird. One afternoon towards the end of the trip, Victoria and I were listening to Nelly in the bedroom and out of nowhere he just flipped out. I remember him busting open the door, shouting that we were listening to "junk" music, and then ripping Victoria's CD out of our little portable player and breaking it in half. He wasn't completely strung out like he had been when we went to stay with him in Kermit, but he definitely looked rough. We hadn't forgotten what happened that time, so we just kept silent and tried to stay out of his way.

An hour or two later he banged on the door again and said to get ready because we were all going out. He said he had to go pick up a friend and there was no one to watch us so we all had to go along with him. I don't think we realized just how messed up he was until we got in the car. We had seen him drinking beers all day, but now we started to wonder if he had been mixing it with pills because he was nodding off and swerving all over the road. He kept saying, "I'm good. I'm good," but he obviously wasn't. It was terrifying. I just kept thinking, "I don't want to die today." Eventually, we pulled into the parking lot of some roadside bar. My dad went inside and after a little while he came out stumbling with some random guy. Then he got back behind the wheel and we drove home. It's a miracle we made it back to his trailer without getting into a wreck.

Just the girls: Me, my mom, and Victoria.

On the day before we were supposed to go back home to West Virginia, Victoria and I went for a walk down the dirt road behind the trailer. I hadn't said anything to anyone, but I'd been freaking out ever since that night Josh came over because I thought I might be pregnant. I knew very little about reproduction or contraception, so it was partly because I didn't know if I could still get pregnant even though he wore a condom every time, but I think I was mostly freaking out because I had sex for the first time and I was scared. Deep down I felt like I had done something wrong and I was going to be punished for it. I confided in Victoria about sleeping with Josh and she said

I better call Mom. My dad had this cordless phone, and I remember pacing in front of his trailer as I worked up the courage to press the numbers for my mom's cell phone. I didn't have any clue what I was going to say.

The second she picked up the phone and I heard her voice, I panicked and just blurted out, "Mom, I need to tell you something, but you have to promise not to be mad at me." Right away, she was annoyed. "What did you do now, Leah?" Her tone was sharp, like it was more of a warning than a question. I instantly regretted calling her, but there was no turning back now.

"I'm really scared to tell you this," I said quietly, my voice cracking, "but I had sex with Josh."

"What! Do you realize you could be pregnant, Leah?"

"I know. I know," by this point I was crying so I hard I could barely catch my breath, "I think I might be. I'm so sorry. I'm so, so sorry."

"Oh, my God, this is ridiculous," she was furious. "I'm coming to get you right now."

As soon as we got off the phone, she called Josh's mom and they drove down to Florida together that same day. I should have known she would be angry. When was she *not* angry? It was her default emotion. But I didn't feel like either one of them was really concerned about *me*. It seemed like it was more of an irritation or inconvenience that they wanted to get straightened out.

Yulee is the first exit off I-95 when you cross the state line from Georgia into Florida, but it was still at least a ten-hour drive from West Virginia, so they had plenty of time to stop at a drug store on the way. The first thing my mom did when they got there was to march me into the bathroom to take a pregnancy test. The only thing she said to me was, "You better not be pregnant, Leah." Then she just stood there in silence, watching to make sure I peed on the stick properly. It was just like when she had me pee in a cup after she found the bag of weed on top of the fridge, except this time, the test came back negative.

Once they confirmed I wasn't pregnant, my mom said, "I'm putting you on the Depo shot as soon as we get back home." She was raised to be afraid to talk about sex and birth control with her mother, so with me she overcompensated (a pattern that would continue as I got older). I think her attitude was basically, *Well, you're sexually active now, so you're going on birth control.* There was no discussion about whether, at thirteen years old, I was ready to be having sex. There was no acknowledgment that maybe by encouraging me to pursue a relationship with Josh she had played a part in pushing me into having sex. Even my dad (who was hardly the voice of reason in our family) chimed in, "What did you think was going to happen, Dawn? She should have never been hanging around with an eighteen-year-old in the first place."

She was angry that I had sex, but she wasn't capable of seeing the bigger, underlying problem. I was already predisposed to lock onto dysfunctional relationships because I was searching for something to fill the void created by my dad repeatedly abandoning us. On top of that, I had been watching my mom needing one man or another to validate her self-worth for years. Whether she realized it or not, I was being conditioned to equate sex with love.

And because I had such low self-esteem, I would end up getting stuck in a pattern of falling for the first guy who paid me any attention because it felt like love and pushing away anyone who did love me because deep down, I didn't feel worthy.

We drove back to Dunbar mostly in silence, and the very next day my mom took me down to the clinic. I took another pregnancy test, just to be sure, and then she had them give me a Depo-Provera injection. Ironically, I was actually practicing safer sex *before* she put me on the Depo because we were using condoms every time. For a birth control injection to be effective you have to get it every three months like clockwork (and it doesn't protect against STDs), so it's definitely not an ideal method of contraception for a teenage girl—a reality I would ultimately have to learn for myself the hard way.

We ended up moving again not long after that. We left our house in Dunbar and moved into a mobile home out on Quick Road in Elkview. I remember standing on the porch of our new place and crying my eyes out because Josh had stopped talking to me. Another girl had come into the picture while I was in Florida. She was the daughter of another one of his mom's friends and a year or two older than me. He started hooking up with her and just ghosted me, which was devastating because I was so naive that I truly believed that I was going to be with him forever. I just remember thinking, *My life is over.*

On top of being totally heartbroken, I also had to face the reality of going back to school. Since my mom hadn't gone to high school she could no longer be considered

Me and Kayla,
freshman year of
high school.

"qualified" to homeschool me, so I had no choice but to
register for ninth grade at Herbert Hoover High School. I
was dreading going back to school anyway, but now I had
started to develop body image issues because the progestin in the Depo shot immediately made me gain weight. I
felt totally insecure and self-conscious. The one blessing
was living only half an hour from Kayla, and even though
we wouldn't be going to the same school at least I was
closer to my best friend.

Towards the end of the summer, I decided to check out
the school website and I saw that they were holding tryouts for the varsity cheerleading team. I hadn't cheered

or worked on my tumbling since my mom pulled me out of Clay Middle School and I had to leave the team in the middle of sixth grade, but it was something that I still passionately wanted to do. I knew there would be a lot of girls at the tryout who had cheered all through middle school and would be way ahead of me, but I figured I had nothing to lose and decided to just go for it. I pulled together a little solo routine and went down to the tryouts with zero expectations.

About twenty girls showed up and the coaches assigned each of us a number. First, they had us show them our jumps: herkies, toe touches, pikes, and hurdlers. I had those moves down. Next, they had us do running round offs and front and back walkovers. I was a little rusty, but I held my own and was starting to think I might actually have a shot. Then the coaches asked who could do tumbling. The girls that raised their hands were sent to a separate line to demonstrate their back handsprings, some of them even had their aerials or front and back tucks. Just like that, the little bit of confidence I had mustered completely evaporated. I started to doubt myself and think maybe I had made a big mistake coming to the tryout. I still felt the sting from being made fun of by the girls on my team in sixth grade for not having my back handspring. At the end of the tryouts, the coaches called us all together to read out the numbers of the girls who had made it onto the team. I couldn't believe it when I heard them call out my number.

Making it onto the varsity cheer team changed everything for me going into high school. Instead of feeling

like a lonely little fish in a very big pond, I was now part
of a tight-knit team of girls who shared the same interests
and goals. For the first time in my life, I felt like I actually
belonged. I quickly became close with two of the girls on
the team, Regan and Alyssa, who I had met on the day of
the tryouts. Alyssa was outgoing and had a big personality. She was small but very strong and athletic. She was
also on the varsity softball and a travel team. Regan was
quieter and more reserved, but once you got to know her,
she was very bubbly and fun.

I definitely struggled in my classes at the beginning
of the year. I remember feeling so lost, especially in math,
because I had all these gaps from missing so much of middle school. But instead of shutting down like I had in the
past, something switched on inside me and I found my

voice to speak up. If I was confused or didn't understand an assignment, I would always stay after class and ask my teachers for extra help. It didn't come easy, I had to work hard, but eventually, I made honor roll and was placed in honors classes. It was such an amazing feeling—going to school every morning and not dreading it. I even made my first friend at Hoover (outside the cheer team) on the school bus.

Even though she was a senior and I was a freshman, Jess and I clicked right away. Every morning and afternoon we'd save each other seats on the bus and chat on the way to and from school. Jess was like the big sister I never had. She kind of took me under her wing and made sure nobody messed with me. She had a car, so on weekends she would pick me up and take me shopping or to the tanning salon. She had a younger brother who was in eighth grade at Elkview Middle School, and she kept telling me she thought we'd really hit it off. I thought it was sweet that she liked me enough to want to set me up with her brother, but I remember thinking there was no way I'd want to date a boy who was still in middle school. Jess was so determined to set us up that she even took me to watch one of his football games. He was obviously the star player on the team, because throughout the whole game I kept hearing "Robbie Kidd: Touchdown" being called out on the loudspeaker over and over again. I was impressed that he was such a good athlete, but I was definitely relieved when we left early and I didn't have to meet him. I didn't know how to tell Jess that I wasn't interested in dating her little brother.

Even though Hoover and Elkview shared school buses, Robbie never rode with us. He had football practice every day after school and had to be picked up, so I figured we'd never have to meet. Then, one rainy afternoon in October, practice got canceled. Our bus pulled up to the middle school parking lot and the second Jess saw her brother step on, she called out, "Robbie, come sit over here next to Leah." I felt my cheeks flush, and I knew my face had turned bright red because he was way cuter than I had thought he would be. When he sat down next to me, I felt butterflies in my stomach. We started talking and it was so easy. I felt like we had known each other all our lives. He wasn't like any guy I had ever met before. He was flirty and funny, but he also had this way about him that made me feel like I could relax and just be myself. I didn't have to *do* anything to get him to like me, he just did.

Robbie was the first person that was consistent in my life, and for a very long time, he was the only person in my life that made me feel good about myself. From the moment we met on the bus that day we were inseparable. At the time, we lived really close to each other in Elkview, so he would ride over to my house on his dirt bike after practice and on weekends or I'd walk over to his. I got really close with his family—I even introduced Jess to my cousin and they ended up getting married a few years later. His mom and dad would take me to watch Robbie's away games. I'd see him out on the field and he'd wink at me. It made me feel like I was the most special person in the world. After my experience the first time, I was afraid to have sex again, so I told him I wanted to wait until I was ready and he was totally fine with it. He never pressured me or made me feel like it was something we had to do. When we finally did sleep together at the end of that school year, it was something that I *chose* to do, not because I thought it would make him love me more, but because it felt right and *I* wanted it to happen.

The summer after my freshman year we moved again. Even though Big Chimney was only five miles away from where we had been living in Elkview, it was like once again the solid ground I had thought was beneath my feet was slowly turning to quicksand. We were still in Kanawha County, so thankfully I didn't have to change schools, but it was far enough that it made it harder for Robbie and I to see each other. I couldn't just walk over to his house and spend an hour chatting with his mom and Jess. He couldn't just hop on his dirt bike and ride over after practice. If I wanted to see him or hang out at his house, I had to ask my mom for a ride—and I never wanted to ask because I felt like she didn't like Robbie or his family. I think she felt threatened because I liked being at their house more than being at home. I couldn't wait for the school year to start. Now that Robbie was going to be a freshman at Hoover, we would be able to see each other at school every day. He'd play football and I'd cheer, and then we'd graduate high school, get married, and live happily ever after. But that next year turned out to be nothing like I had imagined.

At the end of that summer, we had to try out for the cheer team again. This time a lot more girls showed up, and a few of the freshmen coming in were really good.

Right away I was nervous because I still didn't have my back handspring. I had been working on it all year and I was so close, but I couldn't land it properly yet without a spot. I remember being in the gym that day and feeling so proud of myself because even though I was a bit wobbly on the landing, it was the best back handspring I had ever done. I thought for sure the coach would see all the progress I had made and how hard I had been working.

When she called out all the numbers for varsity and I wasn't on the list I was crushed. It was like a scene in a movie where time slows down around you, so I was only vaguely alert when she called out my number as captain of the JV team. My mom had shown up to pick me up just as the coach was reading off our numbers. When she flipped out and accused her of having it out for me in front of all the other girls and their parents. I was too numb to be embarrassed. At the time it felt unfair that other girls who hadn't been on the team the year before had made it onto varsity when I hadn't, but the reality is, any decent coach is going to pick the girls who have the most training and families that are committed to supporting the team. I had neither of those things.

All of my friends from the year before had made varsity again. To help soften the blow, I think, the coach made me captain of the JV team. I could still cheer at high school games with the rest of the varsity team, but I couldn't go to competitions. Girls like Regan and Alyssa had parents who paid for private lessons, helped with team fundraisers, volunteered to help out the coach, and came to watch us cheer at every game. I realized if I was ever going to catch up, I was going to have to find a way to do it myself. I had just turned fifteen so I applied for a work permit and got myself a job. Our new place was walking distance from a little grocery store. I started working there a couple of afternoons a week. I liked working. It got me out of my house and gave me a sense of structure and purpose. But I wasn't just working for pocket money; it was so that I could keep up with all the other girls on the team. There was a gym a couple of miles from where we lived that offered private lessons. As soon as I had earned enough money, I signed myself up. On afternoons I didn't have work, cheer practice, or a game, I would walk the two miles from our house down to the gym to work on my tumbling. For months I tried to balance all of it, but eventually, it got to be too much to manage, and I think I just gave up on believing in myself. I stopped taking lessons, stopped caring as much about doing well in school, and threw myself into the one thing that made me feel good: my relationship with Robbie—but when you put that much pressure on anything, sooner or later it's bound to collapse.

I was still taking honors classes and pulling in decent grades. I was still on the cheer team and going to practices and games—but something was missing. I lost confidence in myself and started coasting through my life. Now that I was seeing Robbie every day at school, I poured all my energy into our relationship. The biggest thing that I wanted at that point in my life was to feel loved by someone, but I was so focused on chasing that feeling that it was like nothing else mattered. My friends didn't matter. Cheering didn't matter. School didn't matter. Nothing mattered except that feeling of being loved. But I was so insecure that any time I saw Robbie talking to another girl it made me irrationally jealous, which poisoned the relationship. Unfortunately, this was a pattern that I would end up repeating over and over again until I finally learned that I was convincing myself I was reaching out for love when I was really pushing it away.

Chapter Five:

FIGHT OR FLIGHT

The impulse to run from danger or stand our ground and fight is a primal force in all of us. When we feel threatened or afraid, our bodies are flooded with stress hormones, our hearts pump faster and our pulses race. The part of our brain responsible for reasoning shuts down and our thinking narrows to three basic impulses: fight, freeze, or flee. Those are useful responses to fear if, say, we find ourselves in the woods face-to-face with a wild animal, but the problem is that those same impulses are triggered any time we're afraid in life. We all have a fear that triggers our fight-or-flight response, and for me, it was (and still is) the fear of being alone and unloved.

It's not a coincidence that my happiest time in high school was before Robbie and I started going to school together at Hoover. When our social lives were separate, I could focus on what mattered most: doing well in school and growing as a person. But once our worlds collided, I couldn't help losing myself in our relationship. The unresolved issues and insecurities that had been eating away at me my whole life began to resurface, and I fell into a pattern of behavior that would come to define all my relationships. That hunger inside me for love was so intense, and the fear of losing it loomed so large, that over and over again I gave in to impulses that made me behave in ways I still regret to this day.

I had earned a spot on the varsity cheer team during my freshman year because I had some natural athletic ability, but then I struggled to keep up because my skill level wasn't advancing at the same pace as other girls. When I got moved down to the JV team, it created yet another crack in my fragile self-confidence. Going into my sophomore year, I was so insecure that I felt jealous of any girl who even looked at my boyfriend. But there was one girl in particular who really got under my skin. She would flirt with Robbie every day at school and then post nasty "away" messages about me on AIM and Myspace. She had a reputation for sleeping with other people's boyfriends, so every time someone came up to me and told me they had seen her all over Robbie in the hallway—it made my blood boil. This went on for probably a month or two and I even tried to confront her in the hallway, but she ran away. She didn't come back to school for a couple of days, but when she did it just started all over again.

When word got around that I had tried to fight this girl, we both got called into the guidance counselor's office. We got a long lecture about the consequences of fighting in school, but it didn't exactly spark a healthy dialogue between us about conflict resolution. She kept right on flirting with Robbie and talking shit about me, and I kept right on letting it get under my skin. When I finally told my mom and my grandma what had been going on, their response was that I needed to fight this girl. My grandma even came down to the school one day and pulled me out of class to tell me that I needed to kick her ass right then and there, or I'd be in trouble with *her*. I had already gotten a warning about fighting in school, and the last thing I needed was to get suspended. I got my grandma to calm down so I could go back to class, but her attitude was basically, "You need to stand up to this girl and if you can't do it in school, then you better do it when you don't have school."

My grandmother had a rougher childhood than anyone I have ever known. She was the middle child of twenty kids and was repeatedly beaten and molested by several family members. She survived because she learned to fight for what was hers with her fists. That's how she had raised my mom to see the world. I think in their minds they were teaching me to be strong and stand up for myself. But I wish someone had helped me understand that I didn't have to fight to hold onto anything. The truth is, Robbie wasn't interested in some silly girl flirting with him at school any more than it mattered what she said about me online. I should have trusted in what I had and held my head high, but my mindset at the time was that this girl was trying to take what was mine and (like a dumbass) I was ready to throw down.

It was maybe a week or two after my grandma came down to the school. I don't even remember exactly what triggered me that day. It could have been that someone told me they saw her sitting on Robbie's lap or it could have been that I overheard her talking shit about me in the hallway between classes. Things like that had been happening almost daily since the beginning of the school year. What I do remember is walking out of my Spanish class and seeing her standing in front of the door to another classroom. Something inside me just snapped and the impulse to fight completely took over. This time, I didn't give her a warning or time to run away. I just walked up to her and punched her in the face. She was definitely shocked, but it only took her a second to fight back. And then it was just an all-out brawl. At some point, we must have fought our way back into the classroom because I remember having her leaned over the top of one of the computers and hitting her over and over again. It was like all this rage that had been simmering under the surface had finally boiled over and I couldn't stop. That primal instinct to protect what I had, took over and nothing else mattered.

In the end, it took two male teachers to pull me off of her. Weeks later, one of those teachers came up to me and joked, "Leah, I was trying to pull you off of her and you punched me in the damn chin. My jaw was sore for days. You're a lot stronger than you look!" I laughed because I was embarrassed, but I knew it wasn't funny. I had beaten the girl so badly that she ended up in the hospital and her family pressed charges against me for juvenile assault. I was suspended from school for three days, I had to see a parole officer once a month for six months, and my grandma had to pay the girl's hospital bill.

After that, Robbie and I broke up and got back together so many times I lost track. He was becoming more confident and establishing his identity as an athlete in high school, and I was struggling to hold on to my own sense of self. He was serious about our relationship, but he was also a normal teenager having fun in high school; the way it should be. His personality was flirty and he liked the attention he got from other girls, but it drove me crazy. So we'd get into fights because I couldn't control my jealousy. My flight impulse would kick in and we'd break up for a little while, but then I'd always end up going back to the relationship. It became this cycle where I didn't feel like I was getting the validation I needed from my boyfriend, so I went looking for it somewhere else. If we were on a break and my friends told me some guy thought I was cute and was interested in me, I was easily swayed because I was afraid to be alone and being wanted made me feel good about myself. That instinct to run at the first sign of conflict in a relationship stayed with me for a very long time, and it always got me into trouble.

The first time I got drunk was during one of my breakups with Robbie. He wasn't into drinking because he was so focused on being an athlete (and I was focused on our relationship), so I had never really partied in high school. One weekend I was sleeping over at a friend's house and her dad was having a party. As the night wore on the adults were doing Jell-O shots, so they didn't really notice when we took a few Smirnoff Ices out of the cooler. I'd never had so much as a sip of alcohol before, but Robbie and I were on a break, so I figured, *why not?* It made me feel warm and relaxed. I had just gotten a brand-new Motorola Sidekick with my grocery store money, and I remember sending a bunch of (embarrassing) texts to Robbie. Then we snuck some Jell-O shots out of the freezer and the rest of the night is a blur. I remember barely being able to walk, or even stand. While the world was spinning around me, I heard my friend arguing with her dad. I wasn't sure what they were fighting about, but I heard her say, "Fine, I'm calling Mom." Her parents were divorced and I think she called her mother to try and play her parents off of each other, but it must have backfired because a little while later she showed up at the house. When her mom saw the state we were in, she was furious. The last thing I remember hearing before I passed out was her mom saying to me, "Just wait until I tell your mother, Leah."

My mom came to pick me up first thing the next morning. I was so hungover my head felt like it was going to split open and I was puking my guts out most of the day. Instead of letting me sleep it off, my mom made me go out and do yard work in the blazing heat as part of my punishment. I was so sick and miserable I thought I was going to die. She also grounded me for a couple of weeks and took away my new Sidekick. I spent the next few weeks hibernating in my room and feeling sorry for myself. The worst part was my friend twisting the story to make it seem like it was *my* mom who had flipped out about us drinking. A rumor went around that if I got caught drinking again at anyone's house, my mom would call the cops on the parents—and people believed it because she already had a reputation for being over the top. After that night, whenever the girls on the cheer team were planning to party, they intentionally left me out.

The irony was that my mom had actually gotten a lot more lenient since Victoria and I had become teenagers. Around the time we moved to Big Chimney, Lee had started working the graveyard shift at the hospital. So, on nights he wasn't home, she would let us have friends over and she'd hang out with all of us. I think because she never went to high school, or even got to be a normal teenager, there was a part of her that felt like she had missed out on something. She wasn't even allowed to talk to boys before she met my dad and got pregnant with me, so she liked hanging out with our friends and being around that energy. Around that time, she and Lee were going through a rough patch. She had started seeing a therapist who diagnosed her as bipolar (with depression and anxiety), but she wouldn't take her meds so she was totally unpredictable. One second she'd be flying high and the next she'd spiral into a dark place. I think she also just didn't know how to handle having teenage daughters, so she'd either be so strict it was embarrassing or she'd want to hang out and act like she was the young cool mom—which was also embarrassing. There was no middle ground; it was always one extreme or the other.

By the end of that school year, Robbie and I were still fighting and I was lonely, so I had started talking to this senior that all my friends thought was really cute. Mike was a total country boy. He was into hunting and fishing. His idea of a fun time was to drive me to his house to pick up this huge, hairy hog that his family had living on their property. It was senior week and the faculty had lost a competition with the seniors, the penalty for which was that the teachers had to kiss a hog. After that experience, I definitely wasn't interested in taking things any further, so I told Mike that I was planning to get back with Robbie. At the same time, I didn't completely discourage him from pursuing me either, because hanging out with him was better than being alone.

In all the times that Robbie and I had broken up, neither one of us had ever actually hooked up with anyone else. Talking to other guys was just a distraction that made me feel less lonely when we weren't together. Then, one night, things escalated so quickly I didn't know how to make it stop. Kayla and my cousin were sleeping over at my house and, since Lee was working a night shift, my mom said we could invite some friends over. We called Mike and he came over with his younger brother, who was the same age as Victoria. We were all sitting around the living room, talking and hanging out, when my mom came into the room with an empty wine bottle and said we should play spin the bottle. At first, it was funny; we were all just laughing and not really taking the game seriously. Mike spun, and I was relieved when the bottle didn't land on me. When I spun, it landed on his brother, so I gave him a peck on the cheek and we all laughed. When it was Mike's turn to go again, the bottle landed on the empty space next to me. There was an awkward pause and he went to spin it again. But, before he could, my mom leaned over and pushed the bottle so that it was pointing right at me. I shook my head and said, "No way," but she started wrestling with me and telling me I had to do it. I was laughing, because I thought she was just teasing me, but then she started pushing both of us towards the bedroom I shared with Victoria. The next thing I knew I was in the room with Mike and my mom was holding the door shut from the other side so I couldn't get out.

I remember feeling cornered, like a trapped animal. I remember the sound of my pounding heart echoing so loudly in my head that it was difficult to think straight. Instead of choosing fight or flight, my impulse in that moment was to freeze. I didn't want to kiss Mike, much less have sex with him, but that's exactly what happened. He didn't force himself on me. I think he was actually as nervous and uncomfortable as I was. At one point he even asked me, "Are you sure, Leah? Because this is weird." I wasn't sure (and it was definitely weird), but I still hadn't learned how to say no. So I just shrugged and said, "I guess." It was easier to just let it happen than to think about why my mom had pushed me into that room in the first place. We were in there for maybe ten minutes and it was the grossest sex I've ever had. He was all sweaty and grunting like that hog we had driven to school in the back of his pickup for senior day. When it was over, I felt totally ashamed of myself, but I knew there was no way I could take back what I had just done. Coming out of that room was the most humiliating walk of shame. I remember my mom laughing as we walked out. Then I think she just lost interest because she went to bed shortly after.

Robbie and I ended up getting back together not long after, but it was never the same between us. I didn't want him to know what I had done. The guilt ate away at me until I couldn't take it anymore. A couple of months later, I finally worked up the courage to tell him. I knew he would be angry, but I wasn't prepared for how hurt he was. After I told him he just kept saying, "How could you do that to us, Leah? You don't really love me."

We never really broke up or had any kind of closure. Things between us just got so bad that we stopped talking to each other. He said he forgave me and we tried to make it work, but I think he just couldn't get past it. By the beginning of my junior year, he was partying more, flirting, and hooking up with random girls to get back at me. Of course, my instinct was to run, so I left Hoover and enrolled at Clay High School where Kayla was. I was there for a couple of weeks, but I was totally miserable. So I went back to Hoover. I thought I could run away from my problems, but it was becoming painfully clear that my problems were running after me.

Chapter Six:

SEVENTEEN AND PREGNANT

I *got pregnant on the night of my junior prom, just a couple* of days after my seventeenth birthday. I had only been dating Corey for about a month. I was happier that night than I had been in a very long time, but we barely got a chance to enjoy being together before life started coming at us at a hundred miles an hour. A few weeks after that night, I took a pregnancy test. Just like that, we weren't just two teenagers having fun and falling in love anymore; we were about to become teen parents. Then, an ultrasound revealed we were having *twins*.

We barely had time to adjust to the reality of taking care of two babies when I started to notice one of our girls wasn't developing at the same pace as her sister. This was just the beginning of our very long (sometimes terrifying) parenting journey together. The crazy thing is, Corey was the only boyfriend I ever had that I didn't immediately start projecting myself into some imaginary future where we were married with kids. I knew right away that what we had was different from all my other relationships, and maybe that scared me a little, so I was happy to take it slow. I still believe that if we had been older and more experienced, if we had been together longer, if we hadn't had so much thrown at us before we had a chance to adjust to being parents, that we would have been able to make it. We were so young, and we barely knew each other when I found out I was pregnant. We knew the road ahead as teen parents would be challenging, but neither one of us was prepared for the reality of having twins and raising a child with special needs. We tried so hard for it to be us against the world, but in the end, the world beat us down.

I still remember the first night I met Corey. I had started working evening shifts at the McDonald's in Elkview. I liked working there; it was fast-paced and a lot of my friends from school and the cheer team would come through, so the shifts flew by. Robbie and I had fallen apart at the beginning of the school year, and I had been dating this guy, Will, for a couple of months. He had also just gotten out of a long-term relationship, so we were both kind of each other's rebound. One night, towards the end of my shift, Will stopped in to pick me up from work with a friend I'd never met before. From the moment I saw Corey, there was definitely a spark between us. Later, he told me that when he saw me his first thought was, "How the heck is someone as pretty as *her* with Will?" I don't think either one of us thought we'd end up dating—and

Spring of junior year, just before Corey and I met. Little did I know that in less than a year I would be the mother of twins and millions of MTV viewers would tune in to watch a reality show about my experience of becoming a teen mom.

if someone had told us that in less than a year, we'd be up to our eyeballs in baby bottles and poopy diapers (times two), we would have thought they were out of their minds.

There's not a whole lot of productive activities for teenagers in rural West Virginia. The big thing to do (at least when I was in high school) was to meet up with a bunch of friends at a Park & Ride, and then drive out to the mountains to go four-wheeling through the muddy back roads. The windier the roads and bigger the mud puddles the better. I knew Corey and my friend, Regan, were kind of interested in each other, so one day after school the four of us drove out to the mountains and went mudding. It was one of those fun, carefree afternoons in high school where you're so in that moment you wish it could last forever. The guys brought a six-pack, so Regan and I chugged a beer before going back to school to cheer at a basketball game. I was definitely tipsy, and the coach was furious when we walked into the gym late and stinking of beer, but it was worth it.

Corey and Regan didn't end up working out, but I had so much fun going mudding as couples that I decided to invite my sister along to ride with Corey the next time we went out. The four of us were riding up in the mountains late one night, and the thing for guys back then was to let their girlfriends have a turn at the wheel. I wanted to drive and hit the mud holes, but Will's truck was a standard so I never got to have a turn. Corey drove an automatic, so when we stopped, I asked him if I could drive his truck for a bit and Victoria and I switched places. We didn't realize it at the time, but that was the moment Corey and I clicked. We were listening to music on the radio at top volume, laughing and having the best time ever. He tried (unsuccessfully) to teach me how to hit the mud holes right. I had no idea what I was doing. As we were coming around a turn, I hit a giant puddle way too hard. I must have driven over a pothole or hit a tree stump because I felt the front of his truck hit something. There was a loud cracking sound. I pulled over and we got out to take a look. More than half of the fender was torn off of his brand-new truck and was lying in the road.

I didn't know Corey then the way I do know. He loved that truck. He had named it Black Thunder. It must have killed him to see it damaged like that, but he just laughed and said, "It's fine, don't worry about it"—which is how I know he was already falling for me that night. Then he tore what was left of the fender off and we got back in the truck. That's when Will pulled up with Victoria. I could tell immediately that he was pissed off. At the time I just thought he was acting crazy, but looking back I think he must have picked up on the energy between Corey and me even before we did. I didn't want to leave Victoria on her own with Will, so I got back in his truck and he tore off without even waiting for Corey to follow. He was driving so fast and recklessly that I was terrified he was going to wrap the truck around a tree or a telephone pole. I kept telling him to slow down, and he finally did when I said I was going to jump out if he didn't stop.

I was so freaked out I didn't even wait for him to pull over; the minute he had slowed down enough I told Victoria to open her door and we both jumped out of the truck. He was shouting at us to get back in, but there was no way I was getting back in that truck with my sister. I told him we'd rather walk the ten miles home than drive with a maniac. He took off, and Victoria and I started walking home. A few minutes later, Corey pulled up. I had forgotten that he had fallen behind us until that moment. He rolled down his window and said, "Get in. I'll take you both home." After what had just happened, I had my guard up. So I shook my head and said, "No thanks, we can make our own way home." Corey insisted, and I realized there was no way he was going to leave the two of us out there on our own, so we finally got in Corey's truck and he drove us home.

After that night, I was done with Will. We never even talked to each other again. I definitely wasn't looking to jump back into another relationship, but at the same time, I couldn't stop thinking about Corey. I knew he felt the same way because he started showing up at McDonald's on nights I was working. He would always come in and order a chicken salad. I'd get myself assigned to work the drive-through window, so while he was getting his salad we could talk back and forth. There was an attraction between us that was hard to deny, but Elkview is such a small town that I knew he had already hooked up with a few girls in my circle of friends (including Kayla and one of my cousins). I didn't want to be another notch in his belt, but the more I put him off the more he pursued me. He would talk to my friends, and they would try to convince me to give him a chance. Even girls I knew that Corey had dated were telling me it was different with me, and that they'd never seen him like that with anyone before. Around that time, I had started working at a dentist's office a couple of afternoons a week filing charts. One day, a big bouquet of red roses was delivered with a note from Corey asking me out on a date. It was so sweet and romantic that I finally agreed to go out with him.

After that, we started hanging out every chance we got. I would go to Kayla's house and Corey would come over and see me there. Or we'd go for a drive in his truck and talk for hours. Prom night was only a few weeks after we started dating, but I didn't go with Corey. He went to Clay for most of high school and then transferred to technical school in his senior year. He had graduated the year

Getting ready and posing for
pre-prom photos.

before and was already working at a local water plant, so I think I think he felt weird about going to a junior prom at Hoover. He did get dressed up to meet up with us and take pre-prom photos with me, but I ended up going to the actual dance with a guy friend. After prom ended, my date took me home so I could change and then Corey picked me up. We went for a drive down Fairfield Road, and at some point he pulled over. We started fooling around. We hadn't slept together yet, but the timing felt right. I was due for my next Depo shot in a couple of weeks, but I had pushed it up to the last minute with Robbie before and it had always been fine so I figured we were covered.

Maybe a month later, we took a road trip to Kings Island (which is famous for being the biggest amusement park in the Midwest) with my cousin and her boyfriend. It was a four-hour drive to Ohio each way, but I love roller coasters so it was totally worth it. We had a blast going on all the rides, but on the way home I felt off. Corey was smoking a cigarette out the window and the smell of it made me sick to my stomach. We had just had this really fun summer day, but suddenly my mood turned foul and I was a total bitch to everyone all the way home. I didn't realize it then but I had double the pregnancy hormones flooding my body, which was making me irritable and irrational. Because I was on the Depo shot, I wasn't getting a regular period, so it didn't occur to me until my boobs were sore and basically everything made me want to puke that I might be pregnant.

A couple of days later, my mom and Lee drove up to Parkersburg to visit some family in northern West

Virginia. As soon as they left, I went out and got myself a pregnancy test. I sat staring at that plus sign on the stick for a solid ten minutes before I pulled it together and called Corey. I was definitely still in denial. I could tell he was freaked out, but he was also very sweet and supportive. I think in his mind he had a stable job and we were in love. The fact that we hadn't been together long wasn't ideal, but my getting pregnant now had just fast-tracked where we were headed anyway. Once I got over the initial shock, the idea of becoming a mother wasn't scary to me at all (at seventeen it should have been, but the truth is it wasn't). I should have been focused on graduating high school and applying to colleges. Instead, I was thinking about how I was going to be the perfect homemaker. I had been taking care of other people my entire life, so it just felt natural for me to step into the role of wife and mother. And I truly loved Corey. I just thought, *It's time to be a mom and a wife. That's my life now.*

Our parents had very different reactions when we told them. We actually drove up to Parkersburg that same day to tell my mom. She pretty much accepted it right away (after all, she was already a mother at my age), but Corey's parents, who were much more rational and practical, had a lot of questions and concerns. Where were we going to live? How was I going to finish high school? Was Corey's income at the water plant enough to support both of us, *and* a baby? Were we sure we were ready for the responsibility? Did we understand that we were going to be tied to each other for the rest of our lives? Of course, we didn't have any clue how to answer those questions—we were teenagers who had barely been dating for two months—but we were all about to find out that figuring those things out was going to be the easy part.

At around twelve or thirteen weeks, my OB sent me to the hospital to have the prenatal screening for Down syndrome. Corey had to work so my mom came with me. They took blood and then I had my first sonogram. I remember the nurse moving the wand around my belly, and then all of a sudden her back got a little straighter. She pointed to the screen. "Do you see what I see?" she said to my mom. My mom squinted at the screen for a moment, and then looked up at the nurse and said, "Oh, my!" I had no clue what they were talking about. All I saw was a couple of blobby circles floating around the screen. The nurse pointed to one of the blobs and said, "See that? That's an egg sac." Then she pointed to another blob, "And see that? That's a second egg sac. Honey, you're having twins." I instantly burst into tears. Then I called Corey at work. He took the news pretty well considering. He told me later that when he called his dad to tell him, he was driving, so he told him to pull over because he didn't want him to get into an accident.

I get the twin gene from my mom's side of the family, only it skipped a generation—my maternal great-grandmother had two sets of twins. I was definitely in shock. The fact that I was having two babies wasn't real until I actually *had* two babies. I had no idea how hard it was going to be, or that I was going to be hormonal as fuck throughout the entire pregnancy. I was pretty miserable to be around when I was pregnant with the twins. The littlest things would set me off. One minute I was fine, and the next I'd either be weepy and emotional or irrationally irritated by everything. I'm sure Corey was wondering what the heck happened to his carefree girlfriend. What made it even more difficult was that any time there was an issue between us my mom felt she needed to be involved. I think me getting pregnant was mostly hard on her because it meant she had less control over me. She got along great with Corey until we got to the point where I needed to cut the apron strings and start building my own life.

I should have known I needed to distance myself from the toxic dysfunction in my home in order for my relationship with Corey to survive the night my mom stood in her driveway threatening to slash his tires with a butcher knife. The tension had probably been building for a while, but it began that day because Corey and I had a disagreement. I don't even remember what it was about—I had most likely overreacted to something because I was so hormonal. I was at my grandma's with my mom, and Corey came to pick me up. He and I worked out whatever our issue was and then we all drove back to my mom's house. That should have been the end of it, but when we got there my mom accused Corey of driving like a maniac (which he wasn't) and said I wasn't allowed to get in the car with him.

We were all standing in the driveway arguing. Then my mom went back into the house and when she came out, she was holding a knife from the kitchen. "If you try and pull out of my road," I remember her screaming at

Corey, "I'll slash your tires." Then Lee grabbed me and wrestled me to the ground so I couldn't get into the truck. Of course, that triggered Corey and he started shouting at Lee to take his hands off me. It was so bad that the neighbors actually called the police, but they didn't show up until after Corey and I had already left. Then we went to his dad's house. I remember sobbing for hours afterwards because I couldn't understand how things had escalated so quickly. I ended up staying at his dad's for a little while, but as soon as things blew over with my mom, I ended up back at home.

Around that time, my mom decided we should send an audition tape to MTV for the second season of a new documentary series on teen pregnancy called *16 and Pregnant*. She had already filled out the online application, so all we had to do was film a short home video introducing ourselves. If they liked our story and we got picked, they'd send a camera crew to follow us around for a couple of months. We didn't really take it seriously, but we figured "why not?" It seems like a million years ago now, but I just remember the two of us sitting on the couch, cracking up the whole time because it felt so silly. My mom told me to look into the camera and say, "Hi, my name is Leah Messer. I'm from Elkview, West Virginia, and I'm having twins," but I could barely get through the line without busting out laughing. Eventually, Corey and I pulled it together. We talked about how we met and the things we liked to do. Finally, she got a usable take out of us. Then she sent off the tape and I honestly forgot all about it.

A couple of weeks later, I went to get my nails done and got a call on my cell phone from a number I didn't recognize. I answered and a woman introduced herself as an executive producer from MTV. At first, I thought it was one of my friends prank calling me, but she assured me that it wasn't and that she was calling to do a follow-up interview. She asked me a few questions and told me that she had also grown up in a small town in West Virginia. At the end of the call, she said that they had never had a set of twins on *16 and Pregnant* and that she wanted me to be the focus of an episode in the next season. My life would never be the same again.

Chapter Seven:

REALITY CHECK

On the day my episode of *16 and Pregnant* premiered, my mom threw a big barbecue at her house in Big Chimney. She invited family and a few of my friends over, and we spent the afternoon grilling burgers and playing volleyball while we waited for the show to air. I was grateful for the distraction. So much had changed in my life since I had agreed to be on the show. The twins were now four months old and Corey and I had both moved back in with our parents. I had gone from naively believing that I would happily transition into becoming a mother at seventeen years old, to actually being a teen mom and facing the possibility of life as a single mother of two.

All day long, I had this anxious knot in the pit of my stomach. We don't get to see any footage or preview the shows before they air, so I had no idea what to expect. Corey and I had said and done hurtful things as we struggled to adjust to life as parents, and the cameras had been there to film some of our worst arguments. I knew it was going to be hard to watch, but I truly believed that however painful it might be it would be worth it, because the goal was to prevent other girls like me from falling into the same cycle of teen pregnancy. Nothing could have prepared me for the reality of being on a "reality" television show. I remember sitting in my mom's living room, surrounded by people who had known me all my life and watching this version of myself on the show that I barely recognized. The whole time I just kept thinking, "It didn't happen like that."

After the episode ended, I went online and my Facebook page was filled with the most hateful and cruel comments from people I had never even met. They were saying things like I wasn't "fit to be a mother" and Corey should leave "that whore and find a good woman." I'm a lot more hardened now to that kind of hate, but this was still the early days of social media and I had never experienced anything like that before. I laid in bed wide awake that whole night, crying. In the morning I had to fly to New York City with my mom to film an after-show interview at the MTV studios in Times Square. It should have been such an exciting moment to meet all the other girls who had been on the show that season, but I barely remember any of it. I had never been to New York before, but instead of taking in the excitement and energy of the city, all I could think about was that I had ruined my whole life.

I think what hurt the most was feeling like so much of what made it into the episode portrayed me as this party-loving cheerleader who was just out there doing all the wrong things. What I was most proud of—finishing school so that I could graduate on time with the rest of my class—barely made it into the episode. With all the honors classes I had taken in freshman and sophomore year, I actually only needed a few credits to graduate. I started my senior year at Hoover while I was pregnant. When it got to be too much for me physically, I transferred to a technical school in Charleston that had an expectant mother's program at the time. The teachers were very supportive. There was even a nurse that came in every Wednesday to teach us about prenatal care and help us prepare for taking care of our babies after they were born. I was there for about a month, and then when I got put on bed rest, they brought me all my work and assignments so I didn't fall behind. It was an amazing program for pregnant teens like me, but since the cameras weren't allowed to film at the school, none of that made it into the episode.

I spent most of my pregnancy on bed rest. Six months in I had started having sharp pains and tightening in my belly. Because I was carrying twins, I already had an appointment with an OBGYN at a hospital in Charleston who specialized in high-risk pregnancies. He ran some tests and then immediately rushed me up to the OB floor because it turned out the pain and pressure I was feeling were labor contractions. I was in preterm labor and I didn't even realize it. I was admitted for three days and they had to give me magnesium, which made me sick to my stomach, to stop the contractions. After that, I was put on bed rest. I spent the next eight weeks feeling isolated and lonely, but that doesn't really make for interesting television. So again, very little of that part of my experience being a pregnant teen made it into the episode.

A few weeks after my episode aired, I flew to New York again to film the reunion show with Dr. Drew. This time Corey came with me and we brought the girls with us. It was so surreal to be sitting next to each other in a television studio talking about whether or not we were going to be able to make our relationship work in front of cameras and a live audience. I kept thinking about the day my mom sat us down on the couch in her living room to film the little home video she sent to MTV after she filled out the online application—and how we could barely get through it without cracking up. We had been through so much since that day. We were in a much better place in our relationship than we had been in months, but I had almost forgotten how much we used to make each other laugh. Neither one of us thought for a second that we would get picked to be on the show, and then when we did, I don't think either one of us fully understood how much it ended up impacting our lives.

Trying to figure out how to be a parent (especially a better one than you had) is hard when you're just a kid yourself. On top of that, Corey and I were also still building a new relationship. During the taping that day, someone in the audience asked us, "Are you guys going to try and work it out and get back together?" I remember Corey talking about how he wanted the girls to have the kind of family where they could come down the stairs on Christmas morning and open up their presents with both of us. Even though he had grown up in a more stable home environment than mine, we were both children of divorce. We wanted better for our girls. We may have been young (and totally unprepared for what life was about to throw at us), but we wanted to give them the kind of family foundation we never had.

Corey and I both thought that day would be the end of our reality TV experience, and that we would fly back to West Virginia and move on with our lives. But after we were done filming, the executive producers came up to us and explained that because *16 and Pregnant* was so popular they were spinning it off into a seasonal show called *Teen Mom*. They had already filmed nine episodes with four girls from the first season. Now they wanted to extend the franchise and create a second show using the same format. Of the nineteen girls featured in the second season of *16 and Pregnant*, they chose me and three other girls (Jenelle Evans, Kailyn Lowry, and Chelsea Houska) to be the focus of *Teen Mom 2*. They gave us a contract and Corey and I pretty much signed it on the spot. The only thing we asked for was that both of us be paid equally. However nervous or reluctant we were to expose our lives on camera again, there was no denying that the extra income from the show would benefit our girls. We had no idea what we were getting into.

What I've learned since then is that reality television has very little to do with reality. The goal of the producers of a reality show is to entertain and part of their job is to create storylines that people want to watch. So your life is being filmed, but then that footage is cut up and put back together to fit a certain narrative. In general, with reality shows how your story plays out over the course of a season depends on the relationship you have with your producer. I've worked with some amazing people who genuinely cared about me and my life both on and off-camera, but there are also a lot of reality producers who will do whatever it takes to get the footage they want. They act like they're your best friend to build a bond of trust and then use that to create situations that will produce maximum drama in front of the cameras. You're surrounded by people you think you can trust, but a lot of them have an agenda and if you're naive you can easily be manipulated. The worst part is that you're being judged by millions of people who have this perception of you that isn't entirely accurate, but once they see something on television it becomes truer than the truth.

Getting chosen to be on *16 and Pregnant* and then *Teen Mom 2* has definitely been a double-edged sword. It changed my life in so many ways, a lot of which haven't exactly been positive, but at the same time, it opened doors for me that I could never have even imagined at seventeen years old. One of the best things to come out of the period that we were filming for *16 and Pregnant* was that I got really close with one of the women on the crew who was assigned to my labor watch. Because I was stuck at home on bed rest for so long, we spent a lot of time together just hanging out on my couch, chatting, and watching football on TV. At one point she mentioned she was having relationship issues with her girlfriend. At the time, that was totally shocking to me. I had never met anyone who was openly gay before. I remember my first thought was that she was going to hell because that was what I had been taught to believe. But the more we talked and I got to know her, the more I realized how wrong my thinking was.

When we started filming *Teen Mom 2*, she came with us and stayed with the show for a few seasons. Eventually, she broke up with the girlfriend she was with when we first met and fell in love with the woman she's married to now. The first time I went to New York and saw them together I thought, "That's what love looks like." It was the kind of love I wanted to feel, the kind I had been chasing my whole life. I think that was the moment I first started to realize that I had never really learned how to be in a healthy, loving relationship because I had so few examples in my own life to look to.

Honestly, I thank God every single day for the show, because it introduced me to the world beyond my small town, which was all I had ever known. It educated me and opened me up to the world. I think a lot of people in rural towns are scared of that. They're scared to venture outside of their comfort zone. They're scared to break out of the cycles they're in because they don't know that there are so many possibilities out there for them.

I was already going down that road by getting pregnant in high school and thinking that becoming a wife and mother at seventeen was the best I could do with my life. Even as I was going through this transformation (seeing the world more, meeting different kinds of people, and being pulled out of that small-town thinking), I was still repeating the same mistakes over and over again. It took a long time for me to break the cycle because breaking free meant that I had to learn to create boundaries. I had to learn to create boundaries with my mom. I had to learn to create boundaries with my dad. I had to learn to create boundaries with so many people that were close to me because they were taking more than they were giving and it was depleting my emotional resources.

I remember flying back to West Virginia with Corey after signing the contract for *Teen Mom 2* and thinking about how lucky we were to have this opportunity. We talked about using the money from the show to move out of our small town and get a place of our own where we would be able to have a fresh start, away from all our relationship history and family baggage. Maybe if we had, we would have been able to take on what we were about to go through together, as a team.

Chapter Eight:

HOPE AND GRACE

If there is one thing Corey and I have always agreed on it's that our daughters, Aliannah Hope and Aleeah Grace, are the world to us. I still remember being in the hospital on the day I went into labor and deciding at the last minute to change Ali's middle name. We had planned to name her Gene, after my grandmother, but now that she was about to come into the world something about it just didn't feel right to me. During those months that I was stuck at home on bed rest, I had done a lot of research on baby names and Hope and Grace always stood out to me. I was drawn to the simple beauty of the message in their meanings—as if some part of me instinctively knew that I needed to gift my daughters with these names so Ali would always have *hope* in the face of the challenges she would face, and Aleeah would have the *grace* to live with gratitude for the strength in her body.

Top: Aleeah Grace. Bottom: Aliannah Hope.

I think I knew the moment Ali was born that there was more going on than what the doctors were telling us. Just after the girls were delivered, I remember hearing Corey asking over and over, "What's wrong with her? What's wrong with her?" I had just had a C-section and I was lying in a hospital bed in this huge operating room. I could hear both babies crying, so I knew at least their lungs were strong. Then Corey came over to me and said, "There something wrong with her legs." I couldn't really sit up or even move much because I was still hooked up to IVs and monitors, so I stretched my neck to look over at where the nurse was swaddling the girls up to try and see what Ali's legs looked like. Even though the nurse kept telling him she was fine, Corey was freaking out, so she brought Ali over to me so I could see for myself. She unwrapped the blanket, and that's when I saw that her legs were stuck up over her head and her hands were hyperextended back towards her elbows. They had swaddled her twisted up like that because they didn't want to force her limbs down before they were ready. The photos we took of her in the hospital are hard for me to look at even now.

Then they took them straight to the NICU and I wasn't allowed to see them until the next morning at 6:00 a.m. I never even got to hold them. It was the worst feeling in the world to be separated from my babies like that. I couldn't even take them home with me when I got discharged because they weren't strong enough to leave the NICU yet. I remember leaving the hospital and feeling like a part of me was missing.

When we asked why Ali's legs and hands were like that, the nurses and doctors at the hospital assured us this was fairly common among breech babies and that it was likely because of the way she was positioned as the bottom baby in the womb. They worked with Ali a little bit in the NICU to try and coax her legs and hands back into the right position. Then when we finally got to take the girls home the hospital hooked us up with Birth to Three. This is an amazing early intervention program, especially for low-income families, because not only do they provide speech, occupational, and physical therapists to work with your child, they help parents navigate the healthcare system. In a lot of cases, mine included, they also offer the kind of emotional support you can't get from your own families.

As babies, Aleeah was reaching developmental milestones (picking her head up, rolling over, sitting up, and

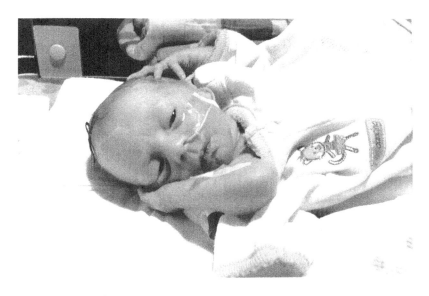

Above: Aleeah in the NICU.

Below: Ali in the NICU (they used a rolled-up baby blanket to help coax her legs back down).

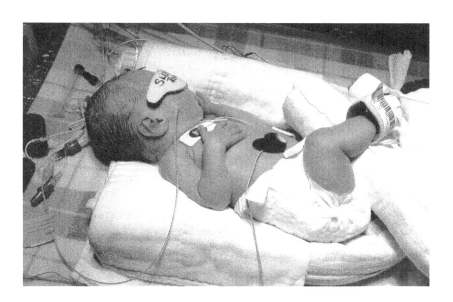

crawling) right on time, but Ali just didn't seem to have the strength. At eight months old, she still had to be in this little baby chair to sit up because she couldn't do it on her own. I knew that just because they were twins, I shouldn't expect them to be developing at the same pace, but as they got older Ali just kept falling further and further behind. By the time they reached their first birthday, Aleeah was walking and zooming all over the house, but Ali still couldn't bear any weight on her legs. Everyone around me was rationalizing that it was because she had more weight on her than her sister (which we now know is because it's harder for her body to burn fat because her muscles are so weak), but deep down I knew something bigger was going on.

For the first three years of Ali's life, I felt like I was holding my breath. We took her to children's hospitals as close as Charleston, West Virginia, and as far as Lexington, Kentucky, where she was tested for everything from a spinal injury to skeletal and neuromuscular disorders. We met with so many different specialists it made our heads spin—geneticists, neurologists, orthopedists, and neuromuscular specialists. They took X-rays of her legs, did blood work and genetic testing, and put her through multiple MRIs—and because she was so little she had to be sedated, which was traumatic for all of us. My maternal instinct was screaming that there was more going on with her than just a developmental delay, but none of the doctors we took her to seemed to be able to tell me *why* she wasn't reaching those early milestones.

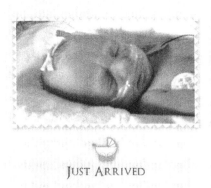

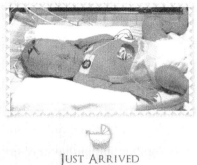

JUST ARRIVED

JUST ARRIVED

Aleeah Grace Simms

Aliannah Hope Simms

When she was around six months old, we took her an orthopedic specialist at a hospital in Morgantown who scared the living shit out of me. I'll never forget the way he poked and prodded her hands and legs like he didn't see Ali as a child but as a specimen in a lab. He clearly had no idea what was wrong with her but instead of admitting that, he started rattling off all these conditions—dwarfism, Down syndrome, spina bifida—that he thought she *might* have without even doing any actual testing. His manner was so cold and clinical that I just burst into tears right in his office. Corey's stepmom was there and she cried right along with me. I just kept thinking, *what kind of doctor says those things to a family without doing any kind of testing?* To add insult to injury, on the three-hour drive back home, I was going through all the paperwork they give you after these appointments, and I saw he had written in his notes that Ali had a lot of "fat rolls" on her arms and legs and that she looked like the "Michelin Man."

Despite how overwhelming and frustrating it was to go through all those tests and still not have any answers, I couldn't shake the feeling in my gut that if we could just figure out what was holding Ali back we could get her the help she needed to thrive just like her sister. But it seemed like the more I pushed to have her tested the more everyone around me (including Corey) insisted that I shouldn't be putting her through it. The only person who seemed to understand why I was so determined to find the cause was Ali's physical therapist in the Birth to Three program. Kim gave me hope when I was feeling hopeless. Even though she had never seen a case like Ali's before, she was on top of it. Unlike everyone else around me, she didn't try to explain it away or dismiss my concerns. She held my hand throughout the whole process and was supportive of my need to figure out what was wrong. She knew the system and would help me find doctors and schedule appointments because I had absolutely no idea where to begin. Ali is still working with Kim to this day, and I'll forever be grateful for all her help over the years.

On my quest to find a diagnosis for Ali, I had to walk a long and lonely road. By the time the girls were about to turn three, I almost gave up. We were still having doctors monitor her progress, but it had been a while since we had done any testing. Then our family doctor recommended a neurologist in Huntington, West Virginia, and

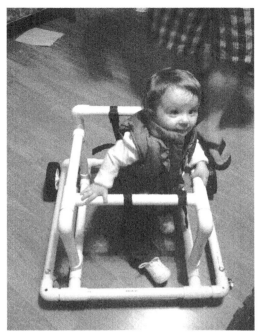

I decided I would give it one last try. If she couldn't tell us anything, then I would do what our families had been insisting I should all along and leave it alone for a while. Maybe it was because she was a female doctor, or maybe it was just the right damn time, but this appointment changed everything. She was the first one to say to me what none of the doctors we'd seen before had been willing to say: She had never seen anything like this before and she was stumped. She then recommended that we take Ali to Nationwide Children's Hospital in Columbus, Ohio, which is one of the largest and best pediatric hospitals in the country.

This meant putting her through more blood work and another MRI, on top of a muscle biopsy (where they took a muscle sample from her thigh and sent it off to a big lab in Boston for testing). It was painful, having to put her through all that, especially now that she was older and starting to become aware that she was different from other children—but for the first time in three years (which felt like twenty) I felt like we were finally moving in the right direction. Immediately after the biopsy, Dr. Tsao, who is one of the best pediatric neurologists in the country, came out to tell us that just based on the color of her muscle (which was light pink, rather than the bright red of healthy muscle tissue) he was confident it was a neuromuscular disease. Then the biopsy confirmed that she had Titin Myopathy, a rare form of congenital muscular dystrophy caused by a mutation in the Titin gene.

At the time, there were only a handful of adults around the world with the same type of muscular dystrophy, and

Ali was the first child ever to be diagnosed. With adults, they know that Titin MD can lead to heart and lung failure, but for Ali, we have no idea what to expect as she gets older because she *is* the research. The process to get to this diagnosis was unbearable. Then, when we finally had it, I was just so angry, because it turned out there was no cure at the end of the rainbow, just more tests and more monitoring. It took me a while, but eventually, I let go of the anger because I realized that knowing what Ali has is our best defense against this awful disease. It also means that she has access to the resources she needs and to the best doctors. We live in hope that the research and discoveries that they are making now, especially with treatments like gene replacement therapy, might one day lead to a cure.

Today, Corey and I are on the same page when it comes to Ali's medical treatment. But for a long time, I felt like his attitude was that she was fine and I was putting her through all that testing because I was looking for something that wasn't there. Looking back, I can see that he was afraid for Ali; it was easier for him to live in denial because facing the reality that our daughter might have a potentially life-threatening condition was terrifying. I think the turning point for him came after the diagnosis when Ali finally got her motorized wheelchair and he saw how freeing it was for her to be able to keep up with other children. But it took years for him to get to that place, and until that moment I felt like I was out there fighting for Ali on my own. I wanted Corey to be on my team, but he wasn't, and that became a wedge that pushed us further and further apart.

On top of everything we were going through with Ali, at eighteen years old I was still looking to fill a void and I brought my "daddy issues" into our relationship. I wanted to love Corey the way that he loved me, but I wasn't capable at that point in my life because I didn't love myself. I wasn't happy with my life and I wasn't happy with the choices I had made. I was lost and I didn't know how to find a path to happiness. I was always chasing after something to make me feel good about myself, and Robbie was like a quick fix whenever I was feeling low. I would get together with him, but of course, it didn't feel right, and then I'd had to live with the guilt and the shame. It was this awful cycle that I was stuck in, and I just kept repeating the same mistakes over and over again. Until finally, I hit rock bottom and got the help I needed to find the love and happiness I had been searching for within myself.

I take full responsibility for the mistakes I made that pushed Corey and me apart, but what people saw on the show was a version of events that was more fiction than reality. To this day I don't believe my cheating with Robbie was the reason our marriage fell apart. About a week before our wedding, I had a bunch of girlfriends over at my mom's, for my bachelorette party. We had all been drinking, and a couple of my friends started texting with Robbie off-camera. Later that night, he ended up stopping by with a few of his buddies. We played beer pong, and by the end of the night, we were all pretty drunk. Robbie hung around after everyone else went home, and I remember him asking me if marrying Corey was what I really wanted. In that moment I realized that

I wasn't sure what I wanted, except to find a way back to that feeling I had when we were fifteen and my life wasn't so complicated. I'm sure he said all the things I needed to hear, and we ended up having sex.

I regretted it instantly. I knew I had made a huge mistake. I didn't want to tell Corey what I had done because I was afraid of losing him and destroying my chance at having the family that I wanted to give our daughters, but in the end, I couldn't live with the guilt. After everything we had been through, I didn't want our marriage to start out with a lie, so a couple of weeks after the wedding I told him what had happened on the night of my bachelorette party. He was hurt and angry, but at the same time, he also understood why it had happened because he had been struggling with the same doubts. Ever since our episode of *16 and Pregnant* had aired, he had been approached by women online and in our hometown. Even though he hadn't actually cheated like I had, he had been out there flirting and enjoying all the attention. We talked and cried for hours. It was one of those relationship-defining conversations where you both admit to the doubts you've had and the mistakes you've made and then come to the realization that what really matters is what happens next. Between becoming parents at such a young age and the weird celebrity status that being on the show had brought into our lives, we agreed that we had both been in a confusing place and decided to try and put all of it behind us and move forward with our lives together.

For the next six months, we were in a really good place. We had been living in this crappy, rundown trailer

next to his mom's house, and the plan was to use some of the money coming in from MTV to move into a better place. I thought we were on the same page, but then he decided that he wanted to wait to move because he wanted to buy a new truck. We argued about it for weeks and I ended up getting so fed up with our living situation that I took the girls and went to stay with my mom. Neither one of us wanted to back down or compromise. I think the whole thing kicked up a lot of issues that had been festering under the surface because what started out as a stubborn argument ended up escalating to the point where we were barely speaking. When my mom told me that Lee had found us a place we could afford, I told Corey I really wanted to take it because I didn't think I could go back to bathing our girls in our mildewy, spider-infested basement. He agreed that we should take it, but then he said he wasn't sure if he was coming with us.

Meanwhile, we were in the middle of filming the second season of *Teen Mom 2*. The film crew was wondering what the hell was going on with us, and once the producers got involved it added more fuel to the fire. I don't know if they reached out to Corey because they wanted to know why we were arguing, or if he contacted them first, but I got a call from one of the producers who said she had talked to Corey and he had told her that we were splitting up because I cheated on him. I was taken aback that this was coming up now, even though we had agreed six months earlier to put it behind us, but she said it was still an important part of our story and Corey had already agreed to film about it. By that point, we were barely speaking, but

Corey sent me a text that made me think that if I agreed to talk about what happened on camera he'd be willing to work things out.

What bothers me about how it all played out isn't that I got called out on the show for cheating on Corey, it's that I felt like I had been manipulated into a situation where it looked like I had been lying to him about it and that's why our marriage fell apart. I don't know what was going through Corey's head, or why he felt like he needed me to confess on national television. I think it was partly because he knew he was going to look bad for wanting to buy a truck over a decent place for us to live, and partly because he was still angry about what had happened on the night of my bachelorette party. I still believe that we might have been able to work through our problems, but once he put it out there that I had cheated he started getting pressure from everyone around him. We had parents involved, we had producers involved, we had an entire show involved, and the next thing I knew he hired an attorney and we were filing for a divorce.

It happened so quickly I don't think either one of us fully understood what we were doing until the day of our court date, and by then it was too late to turn back. We rushed into marriage because we wanted to give our girls a family, and then we rushed into a divorce because we were still so young, we didn't know how to communicate. We never gave ourselves a chance to figure out how to work together as a married couple, so we ended up having to learn to navigate everything coming at us as divorced single parents.

Aleeah, age three.

The next couple of years were really hard on both of us. I'm not sure anyone who hasn't been through what we went through can understand how truly terrifying it is to know that something isn't right with your child, but not be able to find anyone who can tell you what's causing it or how to fix it. Every time we had to have Ali tested, it was like having our hearts ripped out of our bodies, especially when she had to be sedated for the MRIs and the muscle biopsy. In those first few years of her life, I just remember feeling helpless all the time. What we didn't realize until much later was the effect all this was having on Aleeah—who is the only one of the girls we also call by her middle name, Grace. She was such a happy baby and she was reaching all her milestones, so my focus was always on Ali. I didn't get to fully enjoy Aleeah as a baby, because every time she did something like roll over for the first time or take her first steps my first thought would be, *Why isn't Ali doing these things*?

As Aleeah got older she started acting out. She would throw fits, she was hitting, and she would be mean to Ali. This went on for a couple of years until we finally realized that her behavior was stemming from the fact that she needed more of our attention. When they started school, they were automatically put in the same class, and it was a lot of pressure on Gracie because she felt like she had to help Ali all the time. One day she came home from school and I could tell she had been crying. When I asked her about it, she told me that some kids in her class had been making fun of the way Ali walked. She was upset and embarrassed, so she just hid in the bathroom and cried. That's when we realized we had to separate them in school so that Aleeah would have the space to be her own person. I also started taking her out and doing things with her one-on-one so she could have my undivided attention. And whenever we had to drive Ali to see a specialist in Ohio, Corey would take Aleeah and do something special with her.

Even though Corey and I knew intellectually that it was hard on Aleeah, and started working together to find ways to give her more of our time and attention, the emotional impact it was having on her really hit home when the girls were around seven or eight years old. We were filming for the show and out of the blue Aleeah asked me, "Is it my fault?" For years she had been hearing us talk about how the doctors thought the problem with Ali's legs was because of the way she was positioned in the womb. When I was pregnant with the girls, Aleeah was way more active than Ali. I could feel her moving around all the time, taking up a lot of space in the womb, whereas Ali stayed mostly in one position. In her child's mind, when she heard me talking about how they were in the womb, she had interpreted that because she had been the top baby, she had squished her sister and made it so she couldn't walk. It broke my heart that she had been carrying around that guilt all her life.

She's doing a lot better now, but it's still a daily struggle for both of them. I worry all the time that they're not as close as other twins because of everything they have to go through. Ali will see her sister running and doing all the things I have to hold her back from (for her own safety), which is so hard on her. At the same time, Aleeah sees me spending all this time with Ali, taking her to physical therapy and driving to all her doctors' appointments, which can leave her feeling left out and neglected. All we can do is try and find a balance for both of them where

Ali and Aleeah, behind the scenes with the MTV crew.

they know they are loved. With a little hope and grace, they will continue to grow and blossom into the beautiful young women they are meant to be.

Chapter Nine:

FAITH

fter we finished filming the second season of the show, I used the income I had coming in from MTV to set myself up with a place to live and a new car. I had no idea how much longer being on a reality show about teen motherhood was going to last, so my goal was to have the security of a home and a decent car that were both paid off. I didn't have a ton of money, but it was enough to buy a new Kia Sorento and a two-bedroom, 800-square-foot trailer that I fixed up into a cozy home for me and the girls.

I think a lot of people assume that being chosen to be on *Teen Mom 2* was a golden ticket. In some ways it was, because it opened my eyes to the world outside my small town and gave me opportunities I could never have even dreamed of. But there is also a darker side to being in the public eye, and in those first few years, I was totally out of my depth. By that point, the show had gotten so popular that I had paparazzi stalking me in my town (before Corey and I split up, we even had one guy chase us through the back roads until his brakes caught on fire). These guys were so determined to get photos of me that a couple of them found out where I lived and would actually camp out in their cars outside my home. It wasn't hard for them to find me either. Elkview is such a small town that all they had to do was ask around and some friendly neighbor would happily give them directions to my house.

This one night, not long after I had moved into my new trailer, there was a car parked out front. I recognized it because it had been following me around for a while. I was sick of these guys coming to my house, but I had learned enough by then not to talk to them myself because anything I said would end up on some gossip site. My mom and my cousin's wife, Taleigha, went out to tell him to move on. When they came back, they said that he was offering to take me to Target and pay for anything I wanted. In exchange, he wanted to take photos of me while I was shopping and get a shot of me holding a pregnancy test. My first thought was to tell him to fuck off, but then I thought about it and it actually didn't seem like such a bad deal. I had done a lot of work to renovate the inside of my new trailer, but it was pretty much empty because I had left most of my stuff behind when I moved out of the trailer Corey and I were living in and I couldn't afford to buy new furniture. I didn't even have a bed for myself. This guy was going to take pictures of me whether I let him or not, so why not get something out of it for myself?

When we got to Target, I asked him how much I could spend and he said, "Get whatever you want. Load it up and we'll pay for it." After he said that, I wasn't even playing. I walked into that store determined to get *everything* needed. And I did. My mom and I filled up three or four shopping carts with bedding, utensils, lamps, rugs, furniture, a flat-screen TV, kitchen appliances, toys and piles of clothes for the girls. I even got myself a bedroom set. When we got to the register the total was over $5,000. The guy didn't even blink; he just pulled out a credit card and paid the bill. It was so much stuff that I had to call my brother and a few of my cousins to come and help me get it all home because there was no way I was getting all of it in my car. I thought I was so slick—I pretty much furnished my whole place from that one Target shop—but he was way slicker because he probably made five times that much from just one of the photos he had taken.

Towards the end of that summer, MTV flew me and the other girls in the cast out to Los Angeles to film the reunion episode. We had each already had run-ins with tabloid photographers following us around our hometowns, but it was nothing compared to the paparazzi in LA. When we landed at LAX, there were dozens of them already waiting for us outside the airport, and then they followed us to the hotel. When I stepped out of the car, I couldn't even see because of all the camera flashes going off. I don't think any of us were prepared for that. I already struggle with anxiety, and being pursued so aggressively was terrifying to me. I remember thinking, *now I understand why Britney Spears shaved her head.*

That was when the four of us started to realize we needed to hire managers and publicists to help us deal with everything that was coming at us. On that trip, we got hooked up with a woman who wanted to work with all of us. Jessica knew the entertainment world and was really well connected, so we felt like she could help us deal with the press and navigate the industry. One of the first things we learned from her was that celebrity gossip is a business we could turn to our advantage by selling photos and stories about our lives off-camera. At that point, the show was averaging 3.5 million viewers a week (and generating millions of dollars in revenue for the network), but the four of us were all still struggling financially. Finding out that we could leverage all the media attention we were dealing with to bring in extra income was huge. It was a relief to feel like I finally had someone in my corner. I felt like Jessica was taking me under her wing, so I started telling her about things that were happening my life and she would set up articles with celebrity magazines. I thought it was so cool to finally have someone to kind of rep me, and I was so naive I actually thought we were friends.

It was around this time that I met Jeremy. He and Corey were acquaintances through a mutual friend, and apparently, he'd seen us around town together. He had a little crush on me and thought I could do way better than Corey, so when he heard that we were divorced he reached out to me on Facebook. We started chatting on-line, and the first time he called me we ended up talking on the phone for four or five hours. I had never stayed up all night talking to someone like that before. After that, we jumped right into a relationship; we never even officially went out on a first date. Monday through Friday he was working in Pennsylvania as a pipeline engineer, and when he came home on the weekends, we would just hang out like we had been in a relationship for years.

I definitely wasn't over Corey, but being with Jeremy was fun. Every weekend we'd go for rides on his street bike, to the movies, or get tickets to see a concert. I remember going with him to see John Michael Montgomery a week or two after we started seeing each other. When the song "I Swear" came on, I remember looking over at Jeremy, who was really feeling the music, and thinking the universe must be fucking with me because he had no idea that it was my wedding song with Corey. I tried to keep Jeremy separate from the show, but we had just started filming a new season. After a few weeks, the producers said, "Leah, you can't hide things in your life from the cameras. We need to track this relationship." I don't think Jeremy knew what to think about me being on *Teen Mom 2*, but he understood that it was a part of my life. He agreed to let them start filming us together and they staged a very awkward "first date" at a go-kart place to introduce him on the show.

Once Corey saw me settling into a new relationship, he started having second thoughts about our divorce. For weeks we were texting and talking, going back and forth about whether or not we should give our marriage another try. One minute he'd be saying he still had feelings for me and we never should have split up, and then the next he'd back off and say he wasn't sure and wanted to take things slowly. It really started messing with my head. I wanted us to be a family for the girls, but I was also afraid of letting go of Jeremy if Corey changed his mind again. Instead of pressing pause and taking a step back from both relationships to figure out what I truly wanted to do with my life, I dug in even deeper with Jeremy. By the end of October, we had moved in together. When Jeremy proposed to me on Christmas morning I said yes, even though I was still twisted up in knots over Corey.

A few weeks later I found out I was pregnant. After the twins were born, I had gotten an IUD, but it had started

With the twins on Christmas morning, just before Jeremy proposed.

hurting when I had sex so I had just had it taken out. (I didn't know it at the time, but I would eventually be diagnosed with a uterine abnormality that makes IUDs both ineffective and dangerous for me to use as birth control.) I really shouldn't have been shocked that one time was all it took for me to get pregnant again, but I honestly never expected it to happen so quickly. I was devastated. Having a baby with Jeremy would be the end of any chance Corey and I had of making things work for our family. I was sad for myself, but mostly I was sad for our girls. I knew I had fucked up, and I felt like I had ruined their lives on top of mine. What made it even worse was that I ended up having to tell Corey about the pregnancy on camera, which was one of the hardest things I ever had to do. He had come over to pick up the girls while they were filming, and I knew they wanted to film me telling him. He must have known what I was going to say, but when he asked me if I was pregnant, I just froze. I was so terrified of what it would mean for us that I couldn't even say the words out loud, so I just grabbed this little magnetic board that belonged to the girls and wrote the letter Y on it. When he asked me how far along I was, I drew a seven. I knew he was going to be hurt, but I wasn't prepared for the intensity of his reaction. I remember, he just put his hands over his face and broke down sobbing. It broke my heart.

Jessica was one of the few people who knew that I was struggling with how I felt about the pregnancy. We had been talking on the phone regularly since we met in LA, and I felt like she was someone I could trust. So when I found out I was pregnant, she was one of the first people I told. I remember she kept telling me that having another baby was not what I needed in my life. At the time, I thought she was concerned about me losing Corey. Looking back, I think she was more concerned with how bad getting pregnant again so soon after my divorce was going to be for my public image. The more I confided in her about how confused I was, the more she got in my head and I started thinking that having this baby was going to ruin my life. On one of our calls, she told me there was a pill I could take that would end the pregnancy—but I had to decide right away because in a week I wouldn't have that option anymore. I didn't know what to do. Until that moment, I didn't even know you could take a pill to terminate a pregnancy. Growing up in a very conservative, religious part of the country, I had been conditioned to believe that having an abortion was a sin, but I wasn't sure I was ready to have another baby. I needed my life to slow down, but it was like I was on a merry-go-round that was spinning out of control and I had no idea how to get off.

A few days later, Jeremy came home from work for the weekend. Ever since I had told him I was pregnant we had been in a bad place. I think deep down he knew that I wasn't ready to close the door on my relationship with Corey, and he was frustrated that I couldn't let it go so we could move on with our lives. We'd been arguing the whole day, but I promised my mom that we would meet her at one of the schools where she was working after hours as a janitor to help her move some desks. I'm sure that dragging Jeremy out on his day off to haul furniture around an elementary school wasn't helping the situation, but I could never say no to my mom when she wanted me to do something. I was always afraid she would either flip out or cry and say I didn't love her. By the time we got down to the school, we were barely speaking. I remember him standing on the other side of the school desks we were about to move and out of no-where he looked at me and said, "If you're so confused then just take that baby out of you." It was said in anger and I don't think he meant it, but it was the wrong time to say something like that to me.

The minute those words came out of Jeremy's mouth it triggered my flight impulse. I wasn't sure he was the person I was supposed to be with, and I couldn't stop thinking that if Corey and I got back together our girls would have their family back. I told my mom I had been talking to Jessica about terminating the pregnancy. She said she would support whatever choice I made, but if I had an abortion, I couldn't tell anyone what I was doing, not even Jeremy. It had to be done in total secrecy—I couldn't even tell my OB/GYN because he was an old friend of Jeremy's mom—because even a whispered rumor of a Teen Mom having an abortion would be like blood in the water for a tabloid feeding frenzy. She got on the phone with Jessica, and together they came up with a plan to make it look like I was having a miscarriage.

It was a terrible lie, but I think in her mind she was protecting me—and back then my mom probably would have buried a body to protect me. There are a lot of people in our community who believe that having an abortion is murdering a baby, and because I was in the spotlight, I think she was afraid of what might happen if it got out that I had chosen to end my pregnancy. The next day, a close family friend took me down to the clinic in secret. I took one pill while I was there, which they explained would prevent my body from producing progesterone and stop the pregnancy from growing. Then they sent me home with a second pill that would start the cramping and bleeding that would empty my uterus. I thought the fact that I was just taking a couple of pills would make it feel less like an abortion. I was wrong.

I didn't feel anything after I left the clinic, but the next day I took the second pill and a few hours later I started cramping. They told me that it would be like having a heavy period, but it was way more than that. My mom was with me and when the cramping started, she called Jeremy. When she told him I was having a miscarriage, the way she played the role of concerned mother was so damn convincing even I couldn't tell she was lying. The really fucked up part though, was that I couldn't help thinking she was enjoying all the drama. I remember listening to her talking to Jeremy on the phone and wondering how the hell I had let this happen. The pain just kept getting worse and worse, and there was so much blood. At one point, I went to the bathroom to try and clean myself up, and that's when I saw it. At first, I thought it was just another blood clot, but when I looked closer, I could see a sac about half the size of my pinky with an embryo inside of it. I don't think it was real to me until that moment and all I could think was, *what the fuck did I just do?* It was the worst thing I had ever been through.

We had already finished filming for that season so I thought at least I wouldn't have to film about it, but when I called the producers that night to tell them I had lost the baby, they said they were sending a film crew out to my house to film the miscarriage for the show. When they showed up the next morning I was still cramping and bleeding heavily. I had barely processed what had happened, and I was genuinely heartbroken because I had convinced myself I had given up the only boy I would ever have. I hated myself for the lie, but I was in so deep there was no turning back.

I can look back now without regret, but for the longest time, I wasn't okay with the choice I had made. It felt so dark because it was hidden. I wasn't able to talk publicly or privately about it because I let the people who were closest to me at the time convince me that it was something I needed to hide. It wasn't until I was finally able to bring myself to tell Jeremy what had really happened that I started to realize that as long as I was living with the lie it would keep eating away at me. I carried the pain and the guilt around with me for years, until I finally got to the point where I could hold myself accountable for my choices without punishing myself for them.

To this day, I don't know if Corey knows it wasn't a miscarriage. I have to wonder if deep down he knew, but at the time I couldn't tell him. I really thought we would get back together and be a family again, but after everything that had happened, there was just no going back for us. I told myself that staying with Jeremy was moving on, but I think I just settled. He was a great guy, he had a steady job, and the girls loved him. We were happy enough—when we weren't fighting about Corey—and I thought I needed to be married to give my girls a solid family foundation. I was so lost that it didn't even occur to me I could do that for them on my own.

A few weeks later, the girls were with Corey for the weekend, so Jeremy and I decided to have a date night. We had been on an emotional rollercoaster since Christmas, and I thought if we had a normal night out, we could reset and get back to being that fun couple we were when we first met. Unfortunately, that night was anything but normal. We went to see a movie in South Charleston. After it was over, we were walking out of the theater to the parking lot, and out of the corner of my eye, I noticed a group of women who were all looking at me and whispering. I knew they were talking about me, but I was used to that so I just kept walking. As we passed, one of the women, who looked to be about forty, started shouting, "Look at that teen mom whore!" over and over. Being on the show made me a target for all kinds of hateful people, but the worst hate I got was from people in my own community. I kept my mouth shut, but even after we got into Jeremy's truck, I could still hear her calling me a whore.

I should have let it go, but I was sick of ignorant people thinking they could say hateful things to me just because I was on a show. So as we drove by, I flipped her off. That was all she needed to take it to the next level. She came running over, climbed up onto the running board of Jeremy's truck, and started shouting, "Fuck you, bitch!" through the window. I didn't want to be the lead story on TMZ that night, so I said, "I don't know you, and you don't know me. Please just back the fuck off and leave me alone." To which she responded, "Fuck you, bitch!" I could feel a rage rising up from deep inside me like it had when I put that girl in the hospital back in high school, so I took a deep breath and said, "Listen, if you say 'fuck you, bitch' to me one more time I'm going to have to get out of this truck. And I really don't want to. I'm all dressed up and I'm not trying to fight you with heels on." Well, she said it again, and this time when she said the B-word spit came flying out of her mouth and landed on my cheek. That was it. I was triggered.

Later that night, Jeremy told me the moment I looked over at him, he knew from the look on my face that all hell was about to break loose. I knew that if I opened my door hard enough, I could knock her off the running board, so I kicked it open as hard as I could. Sure enough, she went flying backwards onto her ass. Then I jumped out of the truck. She was only a little bit bigger than me, so I was confident I could hold my own if she started throwing punches. Then out of nowhere, her monster ass daughter came bounding over, hollering, "You just knocked my mama over, you fucking bitch!" I was still liking my chances, but then her other daughter came running up and the next thing I knew I had all three of them on top of me. Jeremy got out to try and pull them off, but he left the truck in neutral and when it started rolling forward, he had to jump back in to throw it into park. At that point, the security guards from the theater finally showed up and broke up the fight.

When I jumped out of that truck, I told myself that I didn't have a choice. I was being attacked, so I had to defend myself. But the truth is I didn't have enough faith in myself to choose a better path. I could have risen above the hate and walked away with my head held high, but deep down I didn't believe I was any better than a person who would shout "whore" at me across a movie theater parking lot. I felt like my life had become such a cluster fuck that throwing one more bad decision on the pile wouldn't make any difference. But one bad decision leads to another and then another. My motto at the time was "can't stop, won't stop." Every wall I hit, I just kept going because as long as I kept moving, I didn't have to reckon with the choices I had made.

I rushed into marrying Jeremy for the same reason. I wanted so badly to give my girls the kind of life I never had growing up, but I didn't have enough faith in myself to believe that I could do that as a single mom. The crazy thing is, I had watched my mom settle with Lee because she thought raising us on her own would make life too hard for us (or maybe it was too hard for her), but I couldn't see that I was repeating that cycle with Jeremy. Instead of taking a break to figure out how to have faith in myself to make choices that would put me on the right path in life, I just kept blindly putting one foot in front of the other, hoping it would somehow lead me to a happier place.

Chapter Ten:

RAINBOW BABY

Adalynn Faith Calvert was born during a snowstorm. We were living in a pretty house on a hill at the end of a long dirt road. It was the nicest home I had ever lived in. The twins had the best bedroom and we even had a nursery all set up. For the first time in my life, I was financially stable. I could afford to buy nice things for my daughters and give them all the things I never had growing up. On the outside, it was picture perfect. It was everything I had ever dreamed of for myself and for my girls, but none of it meant as much as I thought it would. None of it made me happy, because on the inside I was broken.

Jeremy and I had gotten married during a small quickie ceremony at a wedding chapel in Catlettsburg, Kentucky (partly because we thought we needed to be married to qualify for a home loan, but then we ended up not even putting my name on the mortgage for the house). A few

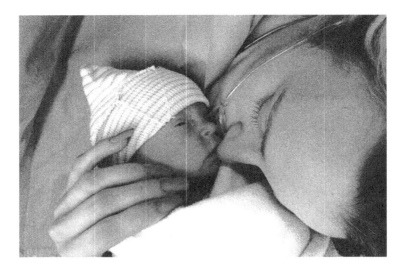

months later, we had a big outdoor ceremony in Myrtle Beach. My dad (who had just resurfaced in my life) walked me down the aisle for the second ceremony. In that moment I was probably as close to happy as I had ever been. It rained on both days. They say rain on your wedding day is good luck, but I call BS on that theory.

Champagne was flowing at the reception, and we partied late into the night. Kailyn Lowry came with her then-husband Javi, and we all went skinny dipping in the ocean. We were drunk as fuck, and Jeremy and I were not thinking clearly when we made the decision not to use a condom on our wedding night. After what I had just gone through, I didn't want to take any chances, so as soon as we got back home to West Virginia I took Plan B. Well, little miss Addie wasn't letting anything—not emergency contraception and definitely not a snowstorm—stop her from coming into this world.

On the night I went into labor, I woke up out of a sound sleep thinking I had peed myself. I jumped up and ran to the bathroom, but it just kept going. Then it dawned on me, *Wait a second. This is not pee.* I called out for Jeremy. He jumped out of bed (butt-ass naked) and started grabbing towels to clean up the mess. I said, "No, I think my water just broke." I was only thirty-five weeks and I wasn't having contractions yet, so I don't think it really sunk in that I was going into labor until he looked at me and said, "Do we need to go to the hospital?"

The snow had been coming down so hard the night before we had to leave our cars parked at the bottom of the hill. It was around 4:00 am, pitch black, and a good quarter-mile from our house down to Jeremy's truck. Thankfully, the twins were with Corey. It was still snowing pretty heavily, and as we were walking down the hill Jeremy kept telling me to hold his hand. I was too proud (and stubborn) to take his help, so I waved him off and said, "No, I got it. I'm fine." But the ground was so icy, and as we were making our way around a steep turn I slipped, fell on my ass, and slid down the hill. At this point, I was still heavily leaking amniotic fluid. It was so different with the twins. With the girls, my water had just ruptured—so towards the end, I thought I was peeing every time I sneezed—but it never fully broke. I was so clueless that I thought it was like popping a water balloon: all the water would come rushing out at once and then it would be over. But no, it just kept on going and going, all the way down the hill. I hadn't thought to bring a pad, so when we got in the truck, I started grabbing whatever I could to put under me.

Other than my bruised pride (and bottom), I still wasn't really in any pain. On the way to the hospital, I told Jeremy to stop at the store so I could pick up some snacks and a Dr. Pepper—I don't drink it anymore, but at the time it was a major craving. I remember when Jeremy called my mom and told her that we were stopping. I could hear her shouting through the phone, "What?! What do you mean you're stopping? She needs to get her ass to the hospital." I thought I had all the time in the world, so we stopped at the Go Mart in Elkview. Jeremy ran in to get my Dr. Pepper and snacks, and then we went on down the road. Well, by the time we got to the hospital I was in full-blown labor. I was bleeding a little and the contractions were coming on so hard I thought I was dying.

With Ali and Gracie, I was high risk, so as soon as we got to the hospital, they sat me in a wheelchair and basically wheeled me right into a C-section. And then I had two babies. I didn't feel anything—the pain came after when they had to stay in the NICU and I couldn't hold them right away or take them home with me. With Addie, when we got to the ER it was maybe five o'clock in the morning and you could tell everything was shut down. My mom was already there and she told them I was in labor, but because I was only thirty-five weeks, they made me wait for them to swab me for amniotic fluid with what looked like a giant Q-tip. Sure enough, it turned dark purple, so they finally sent me up to the labor and delivery floor.

Maybe an hour and a half later, I was still waiting, and then I felt like I had to poop. I wasn't supposed to get out of bed if I was in active labor, but they still hadn't checked me to see how much I was dilated. They left a bedpan, but I told my mom, "There's no way I am using that thing." I was so stubborn. "Well, you're going to have to," she said, "because you can't get up." So, I told her, "I guess they're just going to have to figure it out while I'm giving birth because I'd rather hold it in than poop in this bed. It ain't happening." By that point, my mom (who has no boundaries) was ready to check me herself right then and there, but thankfully a nurse finally showed up to examine me. She took one look down there and said, "Oh, my God. I've never seen a baby's foot sticking out like that before.

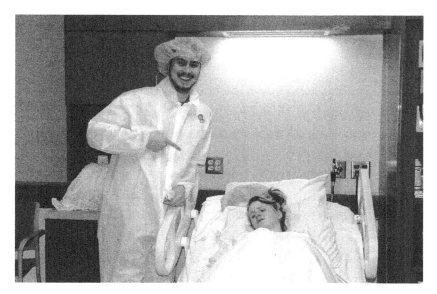

Jeremy is smiling like a proud papa to be, but the look on my face says, "I have a foot sticking out of my vagina and I feel like I have to poop."

Whatever you do, do *not* push. We need to page your doctor and get you into the OR now." All I could think was, *what the hell? I've been here for hours. Why did they let me get this far?*

Before I could have a C-section, they had to do a spinal block, which is where they inject pain medication directly into your spine. They don't let anyone, not even the father, into the OR while this is happening. I was dilated to a seven and my body wanted to push, but I sat there holding very still because I understood that if I moved the anesthesiologist wasn't going to be able to insert the needle properly. The first time I felt it go in, my entire right side went numb all the way up to my head. Then I felt the needle go in again, and the same thing happened on the other side. I can handle pain. I have a pretty high threshold, but this dude just kept sticking me over and over again. As he was doing it, one side of my body would go numb but not the other. Then my leg would jerk or my arm would twitch. It was the craziest thing ever.

Finally, after so many times, I turned to the nurse and said, "Something's not right. How many times does he have to inject me with this needle?" But they just kept saying, "We're going to need you to hold still, ma'am." I *was* holding still, but it was a struggle because I had a foot sticking out of me, my contractions were so close together I could barely breathe, and I still felt like I needed to poop. I was starting to feel truly terrified that I was going to end up paralyzed, so I started screaming, "Somebody please help me," and hollering for Jeremy. When my

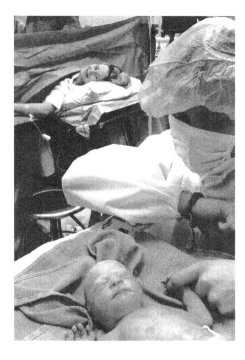

This photo (taken just after Addie was delivered) captures how far away I felt from her during the first two years of her life.

doctor finally came in, I was in tears. I said, "Please, help me. I don't know what he's doing to me."

She said, "You're fine. Everything's okay, Leah. Just relax and hold still." I don't think she understood that this motherfucker had stuck me a dozen times already. I remember hearing him say, "Grab the epidural pack, we'll stick it in that way," and when he injected me the last time, I just felt a warm sensation. They got Jeremy and the next thing I knew Addie was born.

That was the most drugged I have ever felt. Most of it is a blur, but after she delivered Addie, I remember my doctor asking me if I wanted to see my uterus. During one of my sonograms, while I was pregnant, she told me I had a bicornuate uterus. My uterus is shaped like a heart, which is uncommon—of course, because everything in my life is uncommon. It's also why my babies were always born preterm and breach. When she asked me if I wanted to see my uterus, I was so loopy I said, "Sure, why not?" Then she pulled aside the little modesty screen they put across your chest so you can't see them cutting you open, lifted my uterus out of my body, and held it up so I could see. It literally looked like a little bubble heart. I remember looking at her holding my uterus in her hands and thinking, "My insides are probably all jacked now up thanks to this doctor."

After they wheeled me back to my room, they brought Addie in and I got to see her and hold her in my arms. She was a perfect, healthy baby. She had no complications

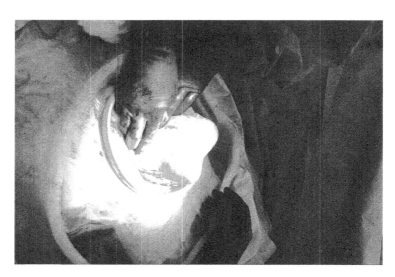

My uterus is shaped like a heart.

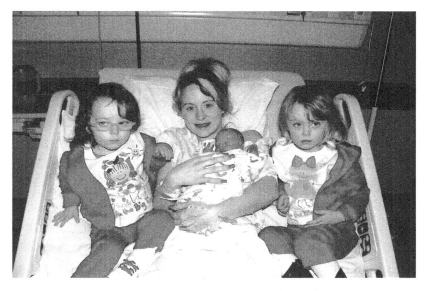

Ali and Aleeah meet their new baby sister for the first time.

so I thought the worst was behind me, but as soon as the numbness wore off, I started experiencing these crazy awful headaches—like my head was going to explode. It was worse than the contractions. The pain radiated all the way down my spine and I couldn't feel my leg at times. It was terrifying. Jeremy went to get the nurse and when she came in, she put me on a morphine IV, but it didn't even touch the pain. When my doctor came in the next day to check me out, Jeremy had to talk for me. The pain was so bad I couldn't even speak. It was a pain unlike anything I had ever felt before. It was coming from deep inside my body.

It turned out that the membrane around my spinal cord had been punctured several times and it was leaking spinal fluid. They did a blood patch, which is where they use a big ass needle to take blood from your arm and then inject it into the puncture to seal it up and stop the leak. They did that twice, and it would help for an hour or two but then the headaches would start all over again. I must have had so many punctures I probably should have stayed in the hospital and had more blood patches done, but after five days I just wanted to go home. I felt like they weren't doing anything to help me, so I told them I was fine so they would discharge me.

When I got home the headaches were just as bad. I was in so much pain I could barely even stand up. When it came time for Addie's first check-up, Jeremy ended up having to take her with his mom. I was so out of it I didn't even realize he had put her in an outfit that was for a three-month-old baby. I remember lying on the couch, feeling devastated that I had to miss my baby's first appointment. Kayla had come over to stay with me and she helped me upstairs so I could take a bath. When she left the room, for some reason I started stripping the sheets off my bed. Then, I couldn't remember what I was trying to do. When Kayla came back and found me lying on the bed without sheets, she said, "What in the world are you doing, Leah?" The next thing I remember was lying in the bathtub with the water still running and suddenly feeling like I was stuck. I started hollering for Kayla to come help me because I was so numb, I couldn't move. It was like there was something wrong with my nervous system and I couldn't control my body.

After the twins were born, they sent me home with a prescription for Percocet. I took it for a couple of days, but then I stopped because I didn't need it. With Addie, they discharged me with refill prescriptions for Tylenol 3 (with codeine), Lortab (which is a combination of hydrocodone and acetaminophen) and Percocet (which is oxycodone and acetaminophen). This time I took them all because the spinal headaches were so bad. There were times during those first few months that Jeremy would have to carry me from the couch to the bed because I couldn't stand up on my own. Eventually, I got to the point where I could function and get through the day if I was taking the pills, so I would take them just to help me get out of bed in the morning and keep going.

For the first year of Addie's life, I was straddling the fence. I was holding it together, but the more I had pile up on me, the worse things got. Until finally, I felt like I was hanging on by a thread. I had married Jeremy because I wanted the stability of a family, but after Addie was born and he went back to work things completely changed. I was so lonely in that marriage. I was experiencing a pain I'd never felt and I needed my husband home with me, but he was gone for weeks at a time and didn't call for days. The reality is, you don't find very many pipeliners that are dedicated to their women back home. It's not the culture. Most of them are out drinking at bars after work, not rushing back to their rooms to call their wives. My grandma had gone through the same thing with my grandfather. He was a trucker who was out on the road half the year, and she found out after the twins were born that he had been living two totally different lives.

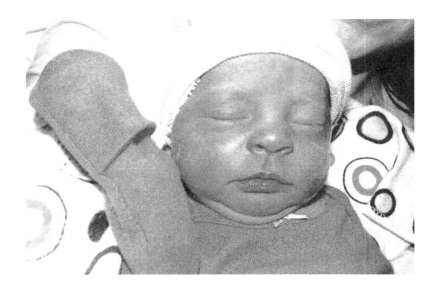

But it wasn't just that Jeremy was gone so much. Having my dad back in my life ended up becoming a major issue in our marriage, which is ironic because Jeremy was the one who had paid for his plane ticket back to West Virginia. He got together with Victoria, and they thought they were doing a good thing by flying him in to surprise me for my nineteenth birthday. They blindfolded me and sat me down on the ottoman in my living room, and the second I opened my eyes and I saw my dad standing there I just burst into tears. I think I was in total shock. I didn't know how to feel. I hadn't seen him or talked to him in six years and he was the last person I expected to find standing in front of me when they took off the blindfold. He stayed with us for a week or so and he seemed to be doing well. Then Jeremy offered him a job working on the pipeline as his assistant so he could move back to West Virginia and be closer to his grandchildren.

My opinion now is that he probably started looking around and figured he had a good thing going. I was on a TV show and my husband was an engineer. We had a nice house, and between the two of us, it seemed like we were making a pretty decent income. Maybe it wasn't his intention to use me, but it *was* his nature. So, he hightailed it back to Florida to pick up his things (and, I assume, to sort out his prescriptions). I remember the day he drove back he seemed super groggy—and, by groggy, I mean I found him slumped over on my couch with food dribbled all down the front of his shirt. I was afraid he had overdosed or stroked out again, so I shook him and yelled, "Dad, are you okay?" He could barely open his eyes, but he mumbled, "I'm just tired, baby." I didn't know what to do, so I just let him lay there. I was terrified because I had already let him bring all his stuff up, and now I wasn't so sure it was a good idea. I had my three girls to think of, but Jeremy reassured me, "It's okay. Don't freak out. He's probably just exhausted from the drive is all." The next day he seemed normal again, so I let it go. But I should have listened to my intuition when it was telling me something wasn't right.

I wanted to believe he'd changed and was doing better, so we put ourselves out there financially to help him get back on his feet. Jeremy gave him a job, we bought him a car, we let him live with us for six months, and when he moved out, we paid his rent. Throughout our marriage, Jeremy and I were constantly fighting about money, but one of our biggest issues was how much I was giving to my dad (which ended up adding up to almost $40,000).

Meanwhile, Jeremy was stressed out at work because he said my dad was out of his mind half the time and never let the pill bottle leave his side, but he felt obligated to cover for him. I knew my dad was going to a clinic in Kanawha City every month and they were filling multiple prescriptions for different opioids, but I wasn't in a good place. All I could see was that I had my father back in my life, and by then I was struggling with my own addiction—though I didn't know it at the time.

I think a lot of the people who got swept up in the opioid epidemic in this country started out like me, taking pain medications that were prescribed to them by a doctor without realizing how powerful or addictive they are. There's such a stigma around addiction that you don't think of yourself as an addict until all of a sudden you realize that you can't tell if you need the pills because you're in pain, or if you're in pain because you need the pills. There are millions of people struggling with opioid addiction in this country, and a third of all opioid overdose deaths involve prescriptions. It's especially bad in rural counties across Southern West Virginia, where "pill mill" clinics like the one my dad was going to handed out opioids like they were candy until federal and state agencies finally started shutting them down and indicting the doctors who had been overprescribing tens of millions of prescription pain pills a year.

I had struggled with depression and anxiety all my life, but once the opiates got added to the mix it sent me over the edge. A lot of that period of my life is just a blackout to me. Even though people will tell me I did things

I don't remember, or I'll watch footage of myself on the show and have no memory of it, I wouldn't go back and change that part of my journey. It led me to a place where I was able to break out of the cycles that had been causing so much toxicity in my life, but it took hitting rock bottom to get there.

It was my girls that saved my life. They were my strength when I felt too weak to fight. They were the light when all I could see was darkness. They were the rainbow on the other side of the storm that brought sunshine and joy back to my life.

Chapter Eleven:

OWNING MY TRUTH

Instead of celebrating what would have been our third wedding anniversary, Jeremy and I were barely speaking. We had been fighting nonstop for so long and we had so many issues, but I kept thinking somehow we could make things work. When he filed for divorce I was devastated. I felt like such a failure. Little did I know, it was going to turn out to be the best decision for me. I had married Jeremy because I wanted the stability of a family, but at the end of the day, you can't force a marriage to work. The universe was telling me it was time to be on my own—I just wasn't ready to listen.

Leading up to that point, I knew something wasn't right with me but I was too afraid to admit I had a problem. Looking back, it seems so clear that I was crying out for help. Unfortunately, the people closest to me were more concerned with either proving I was a bad mother or keeping what was going on quiet than they were that I might be in trouble. The worst part was that the media, and a lot of people who followed the show, had been so cruel and quick to judge, even though they didn't know the full story or what led me to where I was. Meanwhile, I was back to fighting with Corey over our visitation schedule for the twins—when we should have been working together to help both of them navigate Ali's diagnosis—and he had buddied up with Jeremy against me on the show and in the press. I felt more alone than I ever had in my entire life.

I told my mom I didn't like what the medications were doing to me, but instead of encouraging me to go into treatment she insisted that she and my stepfather could wean me off. She was convinced that Corey would use it against me in court if it got out, and she never got tired of reminding me that she would never speak to me again if I lost custody of the girls. I went to stay with her and Lee for a few days, while the girls were with their dads, and tried to quit cold turkey. By that point I had been taking the pills for so long it was hard to tell if I was sick from the spinal headaches or from the withdrawal. They gave me Imodium for the nausea and Tylenol for the pain, but it didn't help. I remember leaving her house and feeling the weight of everything crashing down on me. I just kept thinking, "What am I going to do? I can't lose my girls. Jeremy is leaving me. My mom is going to disown me if Corey gets custody. I'm not going to have anyone."

I stopped in to check on my dad and he gave me Lortab— just to take the edge off. The next thing I remember is driving down Mink Shoals Hill with my foot pressed down on the gas. I was in such a dark place the only thought in my mind was that if I drove my car over the edge it would all be over, and everyone would be better off. Instead, I pulled over to the side of the road and cut the engine. I don't know how long I sat there crying, but eventually, this feeling of calm washed over me and I knew I had to figure out how to get better for my daughters.

When I got back home, I checked my phone. There was another message from Larry Musnik, one of the executive producers on the show. Larry was always on-site when we were filming at a hospital for Ali, and over the years we had grown close. He had been calling because he was concerned about the footage they had of me driving in my car. He knew I wasn't myself and had been trying to get me to go away to a treatment facility in Arizona. I kept saying no because I thought I could handle things on my own, but now I wasn't so sure. I was afraid of how going to rehab would affect the custody hearing, but I knew I had to do something because I had gone from anxious and depressed to suicidal. Larry had already reached out to my manager, Lindsay Rielly, and she had been trying to convince me to go to Arizona as well. When I told her how bad things had gotten, she said, "Leah, you need to go get healthy. I don't see how that's going to make things worse for the hearing. The best thing you can do for your girls is take care of yourself."

In that moment it finally clicked: *I need to get help so I can be the mother my daughters deserve.* It was like when you're on a plane and the flight attendant explains that if you're traveling with a child you have to secure your own oxygen mask first in an emergency. That's exactly what going to Arizona was like for me. I was putting on my oxygen mask, so I could be strong enough to take care of my girls. When Lindsay and Larry stepped in, it opened a door for me that I didn't even know was there. I remember Larry coming over and saying to me, "If you're ready, we'll get you there and support you." I can't thank MTV enough for that. They got me the help I needed when it felt like nobody else in my life had my back.

The first time I went to Arizona I never even made it to the facility. I ended up having to turn around and come right back home. My mom called me in a panic and said Corey was going to file for emergency custody, and if I didn't come home immediately, I was never going to get them back. I had met up with Corey before I left and told him I was going away for a little while to get the help I needed, but instead of feeling supported for taking that step towards recovery, it felt like the focus was getting me to admit that I was an addict on camera. It put me on the defense, so I felt like I couldn't tell him where I was going or why. I was terrified he might use it against me in court. I think if Corey and I had been able to work things out on our own it might have played out differently, but we were both remarried by then and that complicated things—to say the least.

Ever since Jeremy tricked me into confessing that I cheated with Corey a few months after he married Miranda, it had been a shit storm. He was already angry with me for spending the night in a hotel room with

Robbie after my grandmother's funeral, but we had worked through it—or so I thought. Towards the end of our marriage, he came home one night and told me that he had run into a buddy of Corey's at a party, who told him that Corey and I had gotten together. I knew Jeremy had his suspicions, but it didn't even occur to me that he was just fishing. I ended up coming clean about Corey texting me that he wasn't sure about the marriage and that one day he had asked me to come to meet him and one thing led to another. Of course, Jeremy went straight to Miranda. For years after I wasn't allowed to text Corey if she wasn't on the thread.

When I got back to West Virginia, I met with my lawyer and she worked out a temporary arrangement so I could go to treatment without losing custody. Then I flew back to Arizona, and this time I went straight from the airport to the facility. The first seventy-two hours were terrifying. The treatment center was on this huge beautiful campus in the middle of the desert, but when you first get there, they check you into the hospital wing so they can monitor you while your body detoxes. It was such a miserable experience. I had cold sweats, nausea, and diarrhea for three days straight. I tossed and turned every night and all I could think about was how badly I wanted to go home and see my girls. But I started looking around at some of the other people who were there, and what they were going through was so much worse. I met one girl who was coming off heroin. She was having a really hard time of it, but she was so determined it helped me see that we all have so much more strength inside of us than we realize.

After they discharged me from the hospital wing, they moved me into a dorm. Then I met with a doctor who decided to move me from the Addiction track to the Trauma Recovery track. Going to Arizona was the best choice I ever made for myself. Having the space and time to figure out how to become the person that I wanted to be changed everything. I had gone from my mother's house straight into two failed marriages, and I had taken the chaos of my childhood with me into both. For the first time ever, my life had structure. Something as simple as keeping to a schedule made everything feel so much more manageable. It was like going off to college for the first time and having both the freedom and the support you need to figure out who you are as an adult.

Every morning I was up with the sun. I did my laundry or wrote in my journal, and then I went down to breakfast where I picked up my daily schedule out of the basket. We had private and group therapy every day. Then, depending on what track you were on, you might do reiki, yoga, acupuncture, massage, equine therapy, or bio- and neuro-feedback. They taught us about holistic medicine, wellness, and self-care. There were NA and AA meetings for those who needed them, and in the evenings, they had get-togethers by the pool or ceremonies around the big fire ring. My favorite was when we wrote down traumas we needed to let go of and threw the paper in the fire.

The people I met in group therapy changed my life. We were all so different yet we were going through such similar struggles. Every day we sat in a circle, talked about how our days were going, and worked on different lessons. I had always had so much anger around addiction because of my dad, but now that I had gone through it myself and spent time with these vulnerable and courageous people—who were broken but not defeated—I was learning that drug addiction usually has more to do with childhood trauma than the drugs themselves. That's when I really started connecting with my therapist. The more I opened up to her the more I realized that I wasn't just angry at my dad. I remember telling her about how my mom had pushed me into the bedroom with Mike after I wouldn't kiss him during spin the bottle. I kind of laughed while I was telling her, and she told me I did that to disconnect from my emotions as a self-defense mechanism. I realized that all my life I had felt like a puppet on a string and it was time to cut the cord.

The hardest thing for me to open up about was the time my mom made me file a domestic violence protection order against Corey. It was after we split up the first time. We were still just kids and we didn't have an official custody agreement in place. Corey had the girls for the weekend, and when I went to his parents' house to pick them up, he said he wanted to keep them for another night. I went back to my mom's and she said, "You better get your ass down to the police station and file a DVP." She drove me down there, and because I was only seventeen, she was able to file it for me as my legal guardian. Corey had never laid a hand on me, but I think her logic was that it would give me leverage to get the girls back. And

it worked. The cops went out to Corey's parents, took the girls from the house, and brought them out to me. Ali and Aleeah couldn't have been more than six months old, so thankfully they don't remember, but I don't think I realized until that moment how much I hated my mom for making me do that.

It took Corey and me a long time to learn how to co-parent and share time with the girls. We both wanted the same thing, to give them a solid family foundation, and because we couldn't do that together, we ended up in this game of tug of war where everybody ended up losing. I wasn't able to have the girls visit me in Arizona because I was too afraid that Corey's lawyer would try to subpoena my medical records if I told him where I was. It lit a fire under me to do the work I needed to come back stronger, but it hurt being away from them for so long without any contact. I don't know what I would have done if Jeremy hadn't let my mom bring Addie to visit me. I still remember how her sweet little face lit up when she first saw me. We took off running towards each other and I scooped her up in my arms and spun her around. I will never ever forget that moment because it was the best feeling in the world. It reminded me why I was there.

The week before they send you home, they have you ask your family to come in for group therapy to give you a safe space to confront one another and work through your issues. I had done my homework ahead of time by writing a letter to my mom about setting boundaries around our relationship. I remember walking into group, seeing the two chairs facing each other at the center of the circle, and feeling terrified at the thought of confronting my mom. But as soon as I started reading my letter and heard my voice speaking the words out loud, I felt courageous and empowered. I told her that she would no longer have the power to control my life or to punish or correct me or my children again. I don't think my mom knew what to expect when she sat down in that chair. None of us had ever confronted her like that before, especially in front of other people. She was definitely taken aback, but the rule was that she wasn't allowed to respond, so she had no choice but to sit there and listen.

It was one thing to speak my truth into the universe, but I don't think I fully understood the meaning of setting boundaries until I got back home. My therapist knew I didn't have a great support system, so she wanted me to transition out of treatment into a sober living halfway house, but that wasn't an option for me. I needed to go home and be with my girls. They were all the motivation I needed to stay healthy. Now that they had weaned me off the pills, there was no way I was taking that shit ever again. I didn't know if I was going to be okay, but that's where the faith comes in, because I had to take that leap and believe that I could take everything that I had learned and keep growing.

I had nowhere else to go, so after I left Arizona I moved back in with my mom. That's when I was truly tested. It wasn't healthy for me and it wasn't healthy for her. I think her need to control and manipulate me was so ingrained in her that she wasn't even always aware she was doing it, much less able to control it. The only way for us to move forward was for me to truly set boundaries and step away from our relationship. I needed to break free and create my own life. That meant creating boundaries, and not just with my mom. After I got back from Arizona, I took my dad out to dinner and told him I was done with the pills. I was doing better and I really wanted to see him get better too, but if he didn't get help, I couldn't have him in my life. I think he quit for about a month. With the help of his church, he went through a hardcore detox. He seemed to be hanging on and doing okay, but then he went down to Florida for a couple of days and when he came back, he was acting sketchy. Then he got into a disagreement with my brother, took off back to Florida, and I haven't spoken to him since. I had to break free of the toxicity and dysfunction that had defined my life, and that meant

creating boundaries with the people in my life who had been taking more than they were giving.

All I have ever wanted is to give my daughters a better life than I had. Growing up poor, I had confused money with happiness. So at nineteen and twenty, I was trying to buy them all the things I thought I had been missing. As soon as I started getting income from the show, I was like a starving person at a buffet. I wanted everything. I wanted the girls to have the best clothes and the best toys because I never had those things. When you don't have the ability to look inside yourself, it's easier to see what's missing on the outside. Then I went to Arizona, and I had my eyes opened. I realized that the material things I had been craving would never make me feel complete because what I had been missing as a child was structure, stability, and unconditional love.

It took me a little bit to get my bearings, but eventually, I bought the house we live in now and moved way back out into the country again so I could be closer to the girls' school (which ironically ended up closing down right after we moved in because the state got hit by historic floods). I spent a couple of holidays alone, eating a plate of food the girls brought home for me from Corey's. But then, after sitting in that victim mode for a year or so, I started creating my own family holiday traditions with my daughters.

Most people fall into addiction because they're trying to mask the symptoms of anxiety and depression without confronting, or sometimes even acknowledging, the root cause. That was as true for my dad as it was for me. I'm still working on myself, growing as a person, and striving to be the best mother I can be. It isn't always easy. I am tested daily, but if I stumble, I pick myself up again and keep moving forward. I can't control what life throws at us, but what I can do is teach my daughters to live their lives with hope, grace, and faith.

ACKNOWLEDGMENTS

Thank you to Wenonah Hoye and Post Hill Press for seeing my vision and helping turn my dream of this book into a reality.

Thank you to all the fans who have watched my story unfold on the small screen. Your support has kept me going.

Thank you to all who choose to dedicate their lives to changing the world.

I am the person I am today because of the adversity that has come my way.